⋑ *Endorsements* ⋐

What people are saying about *Imagine Living Your Dream:*

"Whether you have a dream to climb Mt. Everest or just lose 10 pounds, Ken Foreman will take you from 'maybe someday' to 'today's the day.' *Imagine Living Your Dream* is an action-provoking read that will light a fire under anyone with a dream in their heart."

— Roma Downey
Star of Touched By An Angel and Producer of The Bible Mini-Series on the History Channel

"Image is the word inside of *Imagine*... and with this extraordinary book, Pastor Ken helps us see that we are all created in the "image" of God; and therefore to imagine is to see, through God's image, a dream so big for our lives that it can only be attained through the help of our Creator. Through his masterful visual ministry, Ken's inner GPS navigates how life-changing dreams were purposefully given to history's great 'imagineers,' starting with Joseph from Genesis and up to today's most influential innovators, to remind us of the transformative power that comes when you surrender to God's dream for your life."

— David Pack
Grammy Award Winning Recording Artist Music Producer

"*Imagine Living Your Dream* is an amazing tool that will stir up the desires deep in your heart to come pouring to the surface. Whether you're 8 or 80, it's never too early or late to discover and pursue the passion that lives inside you. I've always had a passion and dream to play Major League Baseball and win the World Series. By God's grace and never letting up on my dream, I accomplished both feats. But after reading *Imagine Living Your Dream*, I feel God stirring my heart to do more — I can't wait to see where He takes me. I pray this book by my pastor and friend will transform readers to explore and fulfill what God wants for their lives."

— Travis Ishikawa
Member of the 2010 World Series winning
San Francisco Giants

"Anyone in search of guidance on how to merge their dreams and God's plan for their life need look no further. Pastor Ken masterfully captures the essence of how the unique dream God has exclusively for each one of us can be revealed to them. *Imagine Living Your Dream* is a roadmap for those in search of definitive direction on how to reach the destination God has charted out for them, and how to fulfill the unique plan God has for their life. Making your dreams a reality is just a few pages away!"

— Patrick H. Dunkley
Attorney for a Leading University

"Ken Foreman is one of the most guileless, godly pastors I know. If I were lucky enough to live within 100 miles of his church, I would happily drive there every Sunday. His new book, *Imagine Living Your Dream,* is a modern day parable - deceptively brilliant in its simplicity, yet profound and utterly life-transforming. If you've had a dream gnawing at your gut for years, you owe it to yourself to read this book to make your dreams a reality."

— Jonathan Bock
President and Founder
Grace Hill Media

Cardinal Suenens said, "Happy are those who dream dreams and are ready to pay the price to make them come true." Pastor Ken Foreman's book, *Imagine Living Your Dream,* defines the 'game plan' for paying the price to make one's dreams come true. Ken sets the stage for a dreamer to be a doer. I share the reality of the steps Pastor Ken outlines as I see my dream played out with the success of our students at the University Preparatory Academy, a public charter school where students pursue their dream of attending a four-year college or university. We've had three classes graduate with a 99% rate of attendance to four-year colleges and universities. I am deeply inspired by *Imagine Living Your Dream*— Ken is onto something unique and wonderful.

— Jacklyn Guevara
Former Executive Director of East Side Union
High School District
Member of the Founding Team of the University
Preparatory Academy

"My friend, Chris McCormack, two-time Hawaii Ironman World Champion says, 'A dream is a goal with a plan.' Pastor Ken Foreman captures this sentiment perfectly and practically in his visionary book, *Imagine Living Your Dream.* Our dreams are within our grasp, if we are willing to challenge ourselves to dare while committing ourselves to prayer. Realize your dreams - sink to your knees and then rise to your feet!"

— Carl Guardino
President & CEO
Silicon Valley Leadership Group
& Winner of the "CEO Challenge" at Ironman Canada, 2011

"Do you still have a dream for your life? Or have you given up on dreaming altogether? In *Imagine Living Your Dream*, Pastor Ken Foreman will inspire you to dream God-sized dreams again and live the life you deserve."

— Da'dra Greathouse
Multiple Grammy nominated, Dove and Stellar Award Winning Recording Artist and Worship Leader at Lakewood Church in Houston, TX

In the heart of Silicon Valley, where those that dare to dream have changed the world, Pastor Ken Foreman, through his life-changing book *Imagine Living Your Dream*, has found the words to ignite your creative juices, encourage your imagination to soar and help you reap the blessings of your dreams.

— Pat Dando
*San Jose City Council Member
and Vice Mayor &
President/CEO San Jose Silicon Valley
Chamber of Commerce*

"I have been privileged to know Pastor Ken Foreman for over 20 years. He's one of the most creative out-of-the-box thinkers I know. He radiates love and encouragement to everyone around him. I wish I could have read this book when I first started in ministry. In *Imagine Living Your Dream,* Pastor Ken shares practical applications and insights that challenge us to dream BIG."

— Donnie Moore
Chaplain for the Oakland Athletics

I am a visionary so any book about pursuing God's dream for our lives, our families, even our cities and nations, resonates with me very deeply. Pastor Ken Foreman's innovative approach to the story of Joseph in *Imagine Living Your Dream* is a masterpiece and a must read for anyone who has ever had a dream, lost a dream, or longs for a new dream, a God-sized dream. Pastor Ken is the right person to pen this book, at the right time. It will renew hope and inspire a deeper pursuit of the heart of God. You won't be able to put it down!

— Ed Silvoso
Founder and President
Harvest Evangelism, Inc. and the
International Transformation Network

IMAGINE

LIVING YOUR DREAM

IMAGINE! IMAGINE! IMAGINE! IMAGINE!
IMAGINE! IMAGINE! IMAGINE! IMAGINE!
IMAGINE! IMAGINE! IMAGINE! IMAGINE!
IMAGINE! IMAGINE! IMAGINE! IMAGINE!
IMAGINE! IMAGINE! IMAGINE! IMAGINE!
IMAGINE! IMAGINE! IMAGINE! IMAGINE!
IMAGINE! IMAGINE! IMAGINE! IMAGINE!
IMAGINE! IMAGINE! IMAGINE! IMAGINE!
IMAGINE! IMAGINE! IMAGINE! IMAGINE!
IMAGINE! IMAGINE! IMAGINE! IMAGINE!
IMAGINE! IMAGINE! IMAGINE! IMAGINE!
IMAGINE! IMAGINE! IMAGINE! IMAGINE!
IMAGINE! IMAGINE! IMAGINE! IMAGINE!
IMAGINE! IMAGINE! IMAGINE! IMAGINE!
IMAGINE! IMAGINE! IMAGINE! IMAGINE!
IMAGINE! IMAGINE! IMAGINE! IMAGINE!
IMAGINE! IMAGINE! IMAGINE! IMAGINE!

Copyright

Imagine Living Your Dream

Published by Cathedral of Faith
2315 Canoas Garden Avenue
San Jose, CA 95125
www.cathedraloffaith.org

ISBN # 978-1-937514-35-8
© 2013 Cathedral of Faith

Author: Ken Foreman
Production Team: Dawn Foreman, Dr. Wayne Mancari
Editorial Director: Dr. Larry Keefauver
Design: Jackie Tsang

Second Edition 2013

⋗ *Dedication* ⋖

This book is dedicated to the man I most respect —
A leader whose wisdom guides me;
An encourager whose words lift me;
A dreamer who will always be my hero . . .
My father,
Kenny Foreman

Acknowledgments

Imagine Living Your Dream, the title of this book, is my life message. I am living my God-sized dream thanks to:

My wife for 30 years:
Alisa
You have brought out the best in me.
I could never have done this without you.
I'm so glad I get to live my
dream with you.

My parents:
Kenny and Shirley
You are my biggest cheerleaders.
Thank you for shaping the heart of
a dreamer in me.

My family:
Blake, Lauren, Kurt and Dawn
You are encouraging and supportive in
so many important ways.
Thank you for living this dream with me
every step of the way.

My "Dream" Team:

Jackie Tsang, Dawn Foreman, and Dr. Wayne Mancari

You made significant contributions
and worked tirelessly with me on this project.
Thank you Jackie for your creativity.
Thank you Dawn and Wayne for
your insights and edits.

My faithful friends:

James and Debbie Romero

You have stood with me and prayed
with me as this dream has
become a reality.

My church family:

Cathedral of Faith

You help create a place where anything is possible.
I love being your pastor.

Dr. Bruce Wilkinson

Your encouragement brought this book
from a dream in my heart to what you read today.

Dream Releasers
Many others took time to release this dream.
Your thoughtful reads, insights, stories, ideas,
filming, editing and designs were especially valuable.
Thank you for your behind the
scenes investments.

Most of all:

My God

You are the source and sustaining power of all dreams.
Thank you for dropping this God-sized dream in my heart.
You are the ultimate reason dreams come true.
What You have done in me,
do in those who are about to
experience this book.

Table of Contents

Foreword

Introduction: Everything Starts With a Dream   **1**

Section One: Dreamweaver

Chapter 1   Dream On   **7**

Chapter 2   Buried Treasure   **21**

Chapter 3   Navigation System   **31**

Chapter 4   Firm Grip   **45**

Section Two: Pit Stop

Chapter 5   Black Hole   **59**

Chapter 6   Power in the Pit   **65**

Chapter 7   Extreme Makeover   **73**

Chapter 8   Exit Strategy   **83**

Section Three: Desperate Housewife

Chapter 9   On the Job Training   **93**

Chapter 10 Promise Keeper   **101**

Chapter 11 Wind Chill   **109**

Chapter 12 Off the Hook   **117**

Section Four: Prison Break

Chapter 13 Writing on the Wall   **127**

Chapter 14 The aXe Factor   **137**

Chapter 15 Dream Releaser   **145**

Chapter 16 Waiting Game   **153**

Section Five: Royal Ending

Chapter 17 Ready to Roll   **165**

Chapter 18 Problem Solver   **175**

Chapter 19 Forgive and Forget   **183**

Chapter 20 Keep Planting Seeds   **191**

Epilogue: Take A Leap of Faith   **201**

A Personal Note   **210**

The Dream Lives On   **211**

Facilitator's Tips   **212**

Great Resources   **213**

⇒ Foreword ⇐

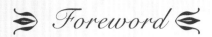

Bruce Wilkinson, Author of *The Prayer of Jabez* •——

Absolutely captivating.
Creative. Inspiring. Humorous. Lifechanging. Authentic. Biblical.
Week after week, month after month, year after year.

Why? Because his messages follow the clear pattern of Jesus and Paul-speaking skillfully to the "right now issues" of our lives, leading us masterfully to the perfect passage. Before we know it, we have forgotten that more than 10,000 people each week also are listening at the edge of their seats—because we are sure Ken has the precious answer to our personal pressing question that kept us up last night.

His style is personal and real-to-life, almost like we are together enjoying an afternoon cup of Starbuck's Cinnamon Dolce Latte, extra hot. How thrilled and touched that someone else knows us so well, accepts us so fully, and has the perfect word kindly spoken just for us.

I must admit I'm not sure how he has done it, but once again, Ken applied his seemingly boundless creativity to innovate by bringing that live speaking experience off the platform and right onto these pages.

Imagine Living Your Dream isn't a printed book, it's an exhilarating experience!

Over and over again, Ken lifts the confusion surrounding how to discover and live the dream— that which you long for in your deepest part of your heart. He uses the word "Dream" to gather together the many related Biblical truths of finding and fulfilling your destiny, of pursuing the God-ordained purpose behind His perfect creation of your life.

You are going to love this book! It's a cross between a magazine, a book, an Internet site, a blog, an ongoing series of tweets, and a personal glimpse of his family's Facebook… all carefully woven to lead you to the life you always sought to find yet seemed to evade you.

By way of a personal note, after recently speaking for a month at the Cathedral of Faith church I must admit, this message has infected thousands! Rarely have I ever seen a church with more people serving God in the area of their destiny with exuberant joy and abundant fruitfulness.

So, if you can unlock the deepest desires in your heart of a walk close to God because you are serving Him precisely the way He created you to be— then grab your latte and turn the page and let your powerful dream out of that dusty cage into the full light of joy unspeakable.

Introduction:

Everything Starts

with a

"I have a dream…"
— Dr. Martin Luther King, Jr., Civil Rights Leader

Everything starts with a dream.

I have lived in the Silicon Valley for most of my life and so, of course, I have an iPhone. When you stop and think about it, the iPhone is an amazing creation. It is much more than a phone. You can find your way around town with it, take great pictures with it, check out your teams' scores on it, listen to the latest sermon on it (hint, hint), and store your favorite music on it. In fact, you can store hundreds of songs on it.

When I was a kid we had these giant circular objects called "records." (If you have never seen one or heard of one, go online and look up "old stuff" and they will show up.) One record contained about ten songs and you needed shelves, and more shelves, and more shelves in your room to store them. With an iPhone you carry hundreds of songs around in your pocket. If you trace the iPhone back to where it came from, there is the store that sold it. There is the place that shipped it. There is the plant that built it. There are the people who designed it, and ultimately, if you follow the trail all the way back, you will find that it all started with a **dream**.

DREAM

Everything starts with a dream.

Every invention ever made, every building ever built, every painting ever painted, every book ever written, every song ever sung, every business ever opened, and every movie ever filmed started with a dream. Follow the trail all the way back and what you see in the visible world began in the invisible world of ideas, visions, and dreams.

"You cannot do it unless you imagine it."

George Lucas
Legendary filmmaker

Everything starts with a dream.

As you make your way through this book, my hope and prayer is it will inspire you to dream. Who knows what God wants to do in your life? It may be a dream to improve your marriage, a dream to get out of debt, a dream to overcome a habit, a dream to start a new business, or a dream toward better health. Before you see a dream on the outside, you have to see it on the inside.

Grammy Award winning singer and songwriter **_Gloria Estefan_** said, "You've got to believe. Never be afraid to dream."

This book will inspire you to dream, challenge you to follow your dream, and give you some important tools to help you see that dream come true.

Throughout this book you will hear about real dreams of real people — some names you will recognize and others you will not. All of them know what it means to discover a dream, pursue a dream, and see that dream become reality. We will follow the story of a man in the Bible by the name of Joseph, who had a dream. There are many twists and turns on the way to his dream. That's usually the way dreams happen—they're never a straight line—there are many twists and turns along the way. As you take hold of his story and his story takes hold of you, I believe it will build your faith as you write your own story.

You can have a dream, you can follow a dream, and the dream God puts in your heart can come true, often in unimaginable ways.

My team and I here at Cathedral of Faith in San Jose, California, have created this unique book that is an interactive experience. It is more than just a book. It includes action points you can complete, videos you can watch, and music you can enjoy. This will be a useful tool for you, and for your friends and family. God is going to expand your imagination and make His dreams for you become a reality.

There are dreams God wants to drop into your heart. There is more He wants to do in you and through you. I pray this book will play a part in seeing that happen in your life. My favorite writer, C.S. Lewis, once said,

"You are never too old to set another goal or to dream a new dream."

C.S. Lewis

Whether you are young or not as young as you used to be, never outlive your dreams. Find a new dream. Follow a new dream. Live your dream.

And above all, make it a God-sized dream.

TRY IT OUT!

Download a free app "QR Code Scan" on your mobile phone, and scan the code bar. You will be able to watch our videos and access other resources.

Try here! Watch NFL great Kurt Warner share about the dream God dropped in his heart.

www.cathedraloffaith.org/kurtwarner

chapter ONE ➡

5

Section 1: Dreamweaver

"Joseph had a dream..."
(Genesis 37:5).

chapter ONE

Dream
on

"Dream until your dreams come true."
— Aerosmith, Legendary Rock Band

chapter TWO
chapter THREE
chapter FOUR

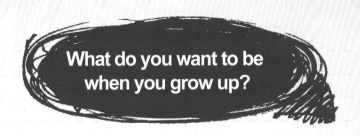

What do you want to be when you grow up?

Do you remember how we used to think about that as kids? We used to think about what we wanted to be. That is a question people ask their kids - a question people ask their grandkids.

One teacher asked her class, "What do you want to be when you grow up?" One boy said, "A fireman." One little girl said, "I want to be a ballerina." Another little boy said, "I want to be possible." The teacher asked, "What do you mean?" He replied, "My mom says I am impossible, and I want to be possible when I grow up."

What if we were to turn that question on its head? What if we were to bring that question into the now? What if your parents, or your kids, or your grandkids asked you that question?

WHAT DO YOU WANT TO BE?
WHAT DO YOU WANT TO DO?

You're never too young or too old to start dreaming. Colonel Sanders was 65 years old when he started Kentucky Fried Chicken— and you can't beat the Colonel!

Never stop dreaming!

Here is another way to think about it:
What would you do if you had a billion dollars?
After you bought the island and sat on the beach
for six months, you might get bored with it. If
money were not an issue, what is it you would like
to do with your life? How would you like to spend
your time? What do you daydream about doing
once all your regular life commitments are taken
care of?

What is your dream?

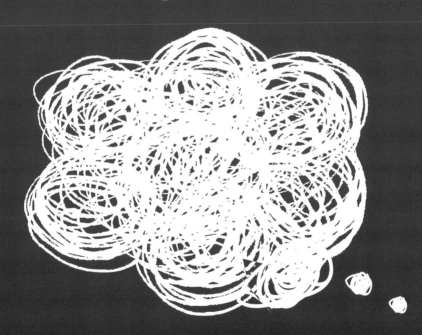

Imagine what it would be like
to live your dream.

**What if you were to find your dream,
follow your dream,
and see your dream come true?**

Maybe you have a dream to go to college.

Maybe you have a dream to write a book.

Maybe you have a dream to get out of debt.

Maybe you have a dream to make a career change.

Maybe you have a dream to start a new business.

Maybe you have a dream to find a spouse.

Imagine what your life would be like if you were living your dream . . .

If you were living God's dream.

"God can do anything, far more than you could ever imagine or guess or request in your wildest dreams. He does it not by pushing us around but by working within us, His Spirit deeply and gently within us" **(Ephesians 3:20-21 MSG).**

Take hold of these words and let these words take hold of you. They can enlarge your vision about God. He has a God-sized dream for you. God can drop a dream in your heart. You may have seen a few of your dreams come to pass, but new dreams are coming from God for you to dream.

"Here is the good news of the gospel: Jesus creates dreams and visions for us."

— **Tony Campolo**
University Professor

➣ *my story* ⬅

I am a member of a partnership working in Quelimane, Mozambique. We are helping people find God's dream.

People in the villages have been down and out since the mid-1970s when their civil war began. It's been hard for them to believe things can be different. We are working with the next generation and they are starting to believe. They are starting to believe they can get an education, they can put food on the table, and they can have better health.

Mission to Africa

They could be the next doctors or nurses, the next farmers, the next teachers, the next lawyers, the next storeowners, or the next city leaders. They are starting to believe they have a God who made them, loves them, and has a purpose for them. Something is stirring in those kids. Jesus is at work in the village creating dreams in their hearts.

There once was a study that was done with fleas. Scientists put fleas in a jar with the top of the jar closed and kept them there for a very long time. Then, they took the lid off the jar, but the fleas would not jump out of the jar. They could jump out of the jar, but they would not jump out of the jar, because they had been conditioned to believe they could only jump so high. The same thing can happen to us— conditioning can put a lid on our dreams. There is more jump in our legs, but we only believe we can jump so high and we don't dream we can jump all the way out of the jar.

Has something put a lid on your dreams?

There are plenty of things that can put a lid on your dreams. Someone may have said you will never amount to anything, or you wouldn't achieve very much, or you've been a loser and you will always be a loser. Those words can put a lid on your dreams. Or, you think you're the wrong age, or the wrong gender, or you come from the wrong family, or the wrong side of the tracks, or you have the wrong color of skin. Those thoughts can put a lid on your dreams. What has put a lid on your dreams? Now is the time, this is the day to turn the page and let God enlarge your vision of who He is and who you can be. Let Him take the lid off your dreams.

He can take the lid off of your dreams.

There was one little girl who grew up in the South back in the days of segregation. Even though she faced racism, this did not stop her from dreaming, imagining what she could be and what she could do. One day, her family was on vacation and they went to see the White House. While they were in front of the gates, a photographer asked if they would like to have their picture taken and so they did. The family posed for a picture in front of the White House. This nine year-old girl looked at her parents, looked at the photographer, and said to them, "One day, I'll be in that house."

Do you know that one day, the little girl, named

Dr. Condoleezza Rice,

was there? She grew up to become the sixty-sixth Secretary of State of the United States and had many meetings in the White House. Jesus is the one who can take the lid off of your dreams.

God can restore your dreams.

Maybe you do not have anything stirring deep down in your heart of hearts. Life has a way of beating you up and kicking you when you are down. It can knock the dream right out of your heart. Perhaps a few broken dreams shut down your ability to imagine. You don't have to stop dreaming. God is the one who can restore your dreams.

Every week I talk to people who say they have lost their dream. You can hear it in their voices and see it in their eyes. Maybe you haven't picked up this book by accident or chance. God wants to help you dream again. God is the one who can breathe life back into your dreams.

Jesus is the one who can restore your dreams.

A young lady in our church family went through a difficult time when her husband passed away. She was at a loss to navigate those days. Her mom was there to help her work through the emotions, make decisions, and live through the implications of her new life as a widow. She attended a class at our church encouraging people to dream again. God started to give her a dream. The support and encouragement which Amy's mother had given her touched Amy's heart so deeply that she began to have a dream.

She had a dream of helping others work through the death of a loved one, through the emotions of grief and the decisions to be made. She took a step of faith, left her job, and began working at a funeral home in order to learn and prepare for a future step to see God's dream fulfilled for her life. She is beginning to dream again. God is the one who restores our dreams, no matter what has caused us to lose them.

My prayer is that wherever you are in your journey, He is going to stir something inside you through what you read and experience in this book.

God can stir up your imagination.

It is time for you to start dreaming and imagining again. Imagine what you could be. Imagine what you could do. Imagine living God's dream for your life. We have a very big God and He is at work inside you every day. He can drop a big dream in your heart. He can stir up your imagination again.

Say this word out loud:

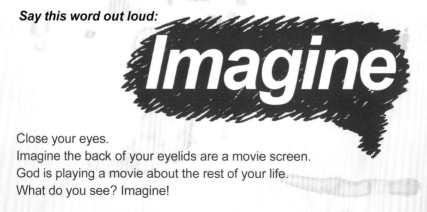

Close your eyes.
Imagine the back of your eyelids are a movie screen.
God is playing a movie about the rest of your life.
What do you see? Imagine!

That is the starting point for living His dream for your life. God is able to do far more than you could ever imagine, and He is at work inside of you. Imagine living your dream. Some people are living someone else's dream for them. Don't live out your dad's dream, your mom's dream, or your teacher's dream. Instead, live out the dream God has just for you. Trying to fulfill another person's dream or vision for you will lead to frustration and misery.

Legendary Martial Artist **Bruce Lee** said, "Always be yourself, express yourself, have faith in yourself, do not go out and look for a successful personality and duplicate it."

Ask yourself, "Am I living someone else's dream?"

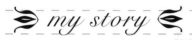
≥ *my story* ≤

"I want Ken to have his own dreams."

When I was a senior in college my dad came to visit me. While he was there, we went out to eat with some of my friends. When I stepped away from the table for a moment, one of my friends asked my dad, "What are your dreams for your son?" My dad replied, "I don't have any dreams for him." My friend was taken by surprise. He knew my dad loved me and was proud of me but at that point it didn't sound like it. Then my dad went on to say, "I want Ken to have his own dreams, not my dreams. I want to get behind him and support him as he pursues his dreams." And for all these years that is what my dad has done. He has been my biggest cheerleader. A big reason I am doing what I do today is because he has believed in me, and believed in my dreams. He encouraged me to be who I was meant to be and do what I was meant to do.

If you want your children to have a fulfilling, meaningful and motivated life, you need to encourage them to dream and pursue their own dream. Then, do what you can to get behind them and their dream. Trying to pressure your children into fulfilling your dream will only create frustration for you and frustration for them.

The movie *October Sky* is based on a true story. In the film, there was a boy whose father was a coal miner. The father expected his son to follow in his footsteps and work in the coal mines. His son, though, had a dream to be a rocket scientist. The father was frustrated with the son. He didn't think it was practical to bank his future on a hobby.

The son was frustrated with the father. To the son, science was more than a hobby, it was a dream in his heart he wanted to pursue. The son went on to enter a science contest with a rocket he built. He ended up winning the contest. His dad got behind the dream and the son eventually went on to become a NASA engineer.

As a parent, one of the best things you can do for your children is to help them dream their dream and follow their dream.

"Train up a child in keeping with his individual gift or bent"
(Proverbs 22:6 AMP).

The word train in Hebrew *(chanak)* means to equip, empower, enable, teach, treasure, and make sweet! Hebrew mothers would wean their babies from milk to solid food with sweet date syrup. Make your child's dream journey sweet!

Have you been trying to live out someone else's dream? Have you been trying to pressure someone to live out your dream?

One of the most freeing things you can do for yourself and for others is to re-imagine what it would be like to live your dream, and what it would be like to encourage others to live their dream. When you are living God's dream, not someone else's, something will stir on the inside.

God is able to do more than we can

He is at work on the inside of you and can drop a dream in your heart. What if we decided to take all we are and allowed God to enlarge our vision of what He could do in us? God is able to do far more than we could ask or imagine. Can you feel something stirring on the inside of you?

Say this word out loud:

God loves to put God-sized dreams in us.

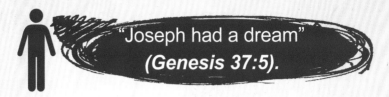

"Joseph had a dream" *(Genesis 37:5).*

That is what happens to a young man in the Bible by the name of Joseph. His story is found in the very first book of the Bible, the book of Genesis. Joseph's story is about having dreams. One night while he was sleeping, Joseph had a very unusual dream (Genesis 37:5).

The custom of his culture was that the firstborn was favored. If there were to be a leader in the family, it would be the firstborn son. Joseph was number eleven of twelve sons. It was very unlikely and definitely not the norm for the eleventh son to have leadership aspirations. No one would have imagined a God-sized dream for Joseph and yet the Bible says, "Joseph had a dream."

He [Joseph] said to them [Joseph's brothers], "Listen to this dream I had: We were binding sheaves of grain out in the field when suddenly my sheaf rose and stood upright, while your sheaves gathered around mine and bowed down to it." His brothers said to him, "Do you intend to reign over us? Will you actually rule us?" And they hated him all the more because of his dream and what he had said. Then he had another dream, and he told it to his brothers. "Listen," he said, "I had another dream, and this time the sun and moon and eleven stars were bowing down to me" **(Genesis 37:6-9).**

This dream Joseph had in the night, became the dream he lived in the day. It was a dream about being a leader. A God-sized dream was dropped in his heart, and Joseph seized it. Something then began stirring inside him.

God wants to begin stirring a God-sized dream inside you, too.

As we follow the story of Joseph throughout the chapters of this book and see how his dream came to pass, let his story take hold of you. It will build your faith as you write your own story.

You can have a dream. You can follow a dream.
The dream God puts in your heart can come to pass.

Who knows, maybe the dream you have will be so big that it will outlive you.

Walt Disney had a dream to build a new theme park in Florida. He bought the land and he drew up the plans, but before the theme park was built he passed away after a bout with cancer. But the dream came to pass. When the park finally did open in 1971, five years after his death, someone said, "It is too bad that Walt could not have lived to see this." The Disney Creative Director replied, "He did see it." He had seen it in his heart, and what was in his heart did come to pass.

He did see it!

Your dream may be the kind of dream that outlives you. But it can still come to pass.

Never outlive your dreams.

Is something stirring on the inside of you?

Dream On

1. Write down any clues you may already have to the dream God has for you:

2. Say these words out loud, "God had a dream for Joseph."
   Now, say it again in faith, inserting your name,
   "God has a dream for _____."

3. Take a few moments to pray this prayer and then add your own
   words to it as you talk to God about His dream for your life:
   Heavenly Father, I thank You that You are the giver of dreams and
   You have a dream for my life. Open my eyes to see and my ears to
   hear what You are saying to me. I commit myself to You and Your
   plan for me. Amen.

chapter TWO ➡

chapter ONE
chapter TWO

Buried
Treasure

"If you can dream it, you can do it."
— Walt Disney, Original Imagineer

chapter THREE
chapter FOUR

After she woke up, a woman told her husband, "I just dreamed that you gave me a pearl necklace for our anniversary. What do you think it means?" Her husband said, "You'll know tonight." That evening, the man came home with a small package and gave it to his wife. Delighted, she opened it to find a book entitled, *The Meaning of Dreams.*

We are walking through the story of Joseph, a man who had a dream for the night that became his dream for the day. Joseph had a God-sized dream. God dropped that dream into Joseph's heart. The dream captured Joseph's heart and got deep down inside of him. In fact, he was so enthusiastic he couldn't wait to tell his brothers the dream (Genesis 37:5). That's what happens when a dream captures your heart. The dream deposited into your spirit ignites a burning desire within you to tell others about it!

Dreams inspire confidence and motivate you. Dreams add value to your life and change your life forever!

Joseph's life would never be the same after he received his God-sized dream. When a God-sized dream takes hold of you, your life will never be the same. God's dream for you will change and transform your life in ways you cannot even begin to imagine. One of the great benefits to a great dream is that it leads to a great life. Not to an easy life, but a great life.

GREAT LIFE

Dreams compel us to just do what must be done. Instead of living life "your way," God's dream for you propels you into doing what God wants you to do in His way. That may not be easy, but it will be great!

> "Always do what's right. This will gratify some and astonish the rest."
>
> ### — Albert Einstein

I have to ask, why would you want to settle for an easy life when a great life is within your reach?

Never underestimate the power of a dream. The same God who is able to do far more than we can ask or imagine is at work in us. He can drop a dream — a God-sized dream — into your heart just like He did for Joseph and my brother Kurt.

GREAT LIFE

WHAT WOULD A GOD-SIZED DREAM LOOK LIKE?

⇒ Kurt Foreman ⇐

My brother, Kurt, is one of the founders of a free, public charter school in San Jose called University Preparatory Academy (UPA). Kurt is the Executive Pastor at our church, and has a heart to serve our community. A few years back, some educators met with him and they decided to create an educational opportunity for students who might not otherwise be able to go to college. It was a lofty dream — **a God-sized dream.**

A God-Sized Dream

One of the first obstacles their team encountered in starting the school was opposition. When applying for the charter needed to proceed in the local school district, they were denied. It was very discouraging for Kurt and his team, but they had a dream, so they pressed on. The economy over the past decade didn't help their cause any, either. School funding in California had been cut, class sizes had increased, but through it all this tiny UPA team persevered. After years in the making, they were finally granted a charter through the local County Office of Education.

It looked like their dream for a quality seventh through twelfth grade school was going to finally be a reality! However, that was just the beginning. It wasn't smooth sailing with budgets, diverse student populations, and the need for quality staffing, but with every hurdle they passed over, the UPA team inched steadily closer toward their dream. Creating a school of that caliber was hard work! It was mind boggling, but Kurt and the team didn't quit.

Fast forward to June of 2012 when the second graduating class of UPA received their diplomas. All but one of the graduates were heading off to college; one young lady was heading to University of California at Berkeley, a young man was going on to UCLA, another was heading off to New York University, and one talented young woman was accepted to our nation's top-ranked Princeton University. It was a glorious day for those graduates and the founding UPA team.

God had given each student their very own God-sized dream, and as Kurt said, "Now students from different economic and ethnic backgrounds will be attending college." God hadn't let them down. God had given each student their very own God-sized dream, and now young people from around the San Jose area are being accepted at the nation's top universities. UPA is consistently putting out top test scores and is ranked at the top among the public schools of our region.

A Focused Life is a Powerful Life

When you have a God-sized dream in your life, it will bring focus to your life.

There is power when you focus. It is an interesting fact that the same light that lights up your house, the same light that lights up the room you are in, can be concentrated and turned into a laser. That light can become powerful enough to cut through steel. A focused life is a powerful life. The focus of a God-sized dream takes your activity and turns it into productivity. I have discovered there is a difference between being active and being productive. They are not the same. You can be active, you can be very active, and yet not be productive. When you take the time, energy, resources, and creativity that you have and you focus them, activity turns into productivity.

The Apostle Paul writes, "I am focusing all my energies on this one thing" **(Philippians 3:13-14 NLT)**. That is what a dream does. It is your dream that shows you where to focus and what to focus on. You can then take your life, focus it like a laser, and make a mark in this world.

"The men and women who have made the greatest difference in history were the most focused."

— *Pastor Rick Warren*
Saddleback Church

When you have a dream, it will stretch your ability.

Several years ago I was taking a Martial Arts class. Part of the class routine was stretching. When I first bent down to stretch, I made it all the way to my knees. Over time I kept stretching; soon I was reaching my calves. Before I knew it, I was able to touch my ankles. And then, miracle of miracles... the day came when I could stretch further and further and touch my toes. When you have a dream, that is what it does, it stretches you. It will stretch who you are. It will stretch what you do. It will stretch what you have. You will have more, you will do more, and you will be more.

A dream will **stretch** you.

Michael Phelps, the greatest athlete in Olympic history, says, "The more you dream, the farther you get." It seems to me he is right. You can stretch a lot further than you think.

Having a God-sized dream will build character in your life.

As you are busy working on the dream, God is busy working on you. He is busy building your character. Perhaps you have a dream to get out of debt. That is a good dream to have.

"The borrower is a servant to the lender" **(Proverbs 22:7).**

You may be so far in debt that you feel like a slave. You are up to your ears in debt, and under a lot of financial stress. Take hold of a dream to get out of debt and develop a plan. As you work toward your dream, you are building —

**A dream is one of the tools
God uses to build His character in you.**

*If you would like to learn more about getting out of debt
please visit page 213 for additional resources.*

A dream can shake off the boredom in your life.

If you feel bored with your life, (I didn't say you are bored with your wife - that is a subject for another book), one of the best things you could do is to take hold of a big, bold dream. Maybe you feel like you are sleepwalking day after day after day. When I was young we used to pray, "If I should die before I wake," but as adults maybe we should pray, "Wake me up before I die." Life is too short to sleepwalk through it and a big, bold dream will wake you up and make you feel fully alive. Make sure it is a big, bold dream. It is much more exciting to shoot for the stars and hit the top of the mountain than shoot for the top of the mountain and hit a telephone post. As you write down that big, bold dream, you will feel your heart start to pound and your blood start to pump.

27

You need a big, bold dream so big and so bold that without the help of God, there is no way you can reach it.

That is why it needs to be a God-sized dream. If you are bored with your life, one of the best ways to shake off the boredom is to take hold of a God-sized dream and let that God-sized dream take hold of you. As you write down that God-sized dream, it will take your breath away, and breathe life back into you.

 ## A dream in your heart will intercept the Law of Entropy, one of the unavoidable tendencies of life.

There is a law of thermodynamics called the Law of Entropy which states, "Everything left to itself has a tendency to deteriorate." Let's take your backyard as an example. If you do not tend to your backyard, if you just let it go and ignore it, it will deteriorate. You do not have to make your backyard deteriorate. All you have to do is to leave it alone and watch what happens (I can speak from personal experience). The same is true in much of your life. You do not have to make it deteriorate, all you have to do is leave it alone. It will go down all by itself.

When you take hold of and go after that dream, you intercept the Law of Entropy. Let's say you have not taken proper care of your body. Have you noticed it will deteriorate all by itself? (I speak again from personal experience.) Then, you get a dream that you want to improve your health. When you do, you are going to take better care of your body. You are going to eat a little healthier. You are going to exercise a little more. You are going to get a little more rest.

"Honor God with your body" **(1 Corinthians 6:20).**

When you give your body some attention, it helps to intercept the Law of Entropy. Where do you need to intercept that law in your life?

What Keeps Us From Following A Dream?

With all of the good things that happen when people start dreaming, what is it that keeps us from finding and then following that dream? I think that the biggest reason is a four-letter word, F-E-A-R. Fear is a very powerful emotion, especially the fear of failure.

The fear of failure can keep us from dreaming at all until we realize that the only people who never fail are the people who never try. We can come back from failure.

Failure is never fun, and yet failure is never final.

In Matthew 25, we read a parable Jesus told of a man who was given a certain amount of money to manage. The man took the money and buried it in the ground. Fear kept him from investing the money. He played it safe. According to Jesus, he played it too safe. That is the biggest failure of all. At the end of the day, it is better to try something and fail than to try nothing and succeed.

In one of my favorite posters

Michael Jordan, the legendary basketball player, says, "I have missed more than 9000 shots in my career. I have lost almost 300 games. 26 times, I have been trusted to take the game winning shot and missed. I have failed over and over again in my life and that is why I succeed."

The ball is in your hands -- take the shot, live the dream.

Buried Treasure

1. Think about the last time you saw a dream come to pass.
   List some of the best things that came out of that experience.

2. A dream is like a magnet. A magnet has the property of attraction. It pulls things toward itself. The same thing is true of a dream. A dream is like a magnetic force that pulls and draws us toward it. What do you tend to be drawn toward?

DREAM

3. Is there a place where fear is holding you back? Write down the word *fear* in small letters and the word *God* in big letters. Know that God is bigger than your fears.

4. Pray this prayer:

   God, I am ready for You to drop a dream in my heart. Thank You for all of the things You are going to do in my life as I find and follow that dream. I will not let fear hold me back. With Your help and with Your strength, I can do all that You want me to do and be all that You want me to be. Amen.

chapter THREE ➡

- chapter ONE
- chapter TWO
- **chapter THREE**

Navigation System

"Keep your feet on the ground and keep reaching for the stars."
— Casey Kasem, American Top 40 Radio Host

- chapter FOUR

A dream for your life may be starting to stir inside you. You want to take hold of that dream and you want that dream to take hold of you. How does that happen? How can you find a God-sized dream? Joseph had a dream in the night that he began to live in the day, but that kind of thing has never happened to you.

You may have had dreams at night about spiders chasing you, flying through the sky on your bike, or speaking to an audience in your underwear (now that's what I call a nightmare). You may have had these kinds of dreams at night, but not the kind of dream that becomes your reality in the day. What can you do to put yourself in position to receive what God wants to drop into your heart? There is not an exact formula for this. A dream can be dropped into your heart in many different ways and places.

One man I know went off to college. He was not into acting, and had never really thought about acting. While he was in a theater watching a movie, God dropped a dream into his heart to become an actor. "The film ended and I heard a voice," he told our congregation one weekend. "It was very clear, I heard it right here (he pointed to his heart) and it was 'I'd like you to be an actor.' So, everyday I'd wake up and it was like I had a mark on my soul. 'I'd like you to be an actor.'"

He took hold of that dream and that dream took hold of him. He went on to become a great actor and starred in many movies and television shows including *The Count of Monte Cristo*, *The Passion of the Christ* and *Person of Interest*. His name is **Jim Caviezel**.

Positioning Yourself to Receive Your God-sized Dream

There are many different ways and many different places God may drop a dream in your heart. Here are a few suggestions that can get you started and can put you in position to receive.

 ## Surrender your life to God.

What if you were to take your whole life, not some of your life, not most of your life, but if you were to take your whole life and dedicate it to God? Are you willing to do whatever He wants you to do? Will you go wherever He wants you to go? Will you be whatever He wants you to be? After all, everything you have belongs to Him. Every day you have belongs to Him. Every breath you have belongs to Him. Finding that God-sized dream can start as you surrender your life completely and totally to Him.

Pray for what God wants,
not what you want in life.

The Bible says, "Offer yourselves as a living sacrifice to God, dedicated to his service and pleasing to him... Do not conform yourselves to the standards of this world, but let God transform you... you will be able to know the will of God — what is good and is pleasing to him and is perfect." **(Romans 12:1-2 GNT).**

If you want to know what the will of God is for your life, if you want Him to drop a God-sized dream in your heart, this is a good place to start—surrender. Surrender your thoughts, feelings and actions to Christ so that you can be transformed from being self-centered to living for Him and others. You will become a servant leader not only realizing your own dreams but also helping others realize theirs.

Can a person have a dream and pursue a dream without God? Sure they can—it happens all the time. But the question I have is: "Why would you want to?" There is a God who loves you and made you and has a dream for your life. That's right—the God who made the whole universe also made a dream customized for you. It seems to me the best thing to do is to surrender your life to Him.

When you find His dream and follow His dream —
that's when you start really living the dream.

What does it mean to "surrender?"
Surrendering is like taking a blank piece of paper,
handing the pen to God, and asking Him to write down
whatever He wants.

Sometimes we fill up a page with the dreams we have, the plans we have made, and the goals we have set. Then we invite God to be part of our dreams. It is different when we bring a blank page to God, and we ask Him to fill the page with His dreams. He doesn't become part of our dream. We become part of His dream. We ask Him to fill the page any way He wants.

Say, "God, you have free reign in my life. I want Your
dream to be my dream." Who holds the pen in your life?

➡ Always start with the "What" question. What is the dream God has for you?

Several years ago, I had lunch with one of the top spiritual leaders in the nation. Throughout the years, he has been involved in many major works for the Kingdom. I will never forget one of the most important things he told me. He said, "Start with the 'What' question: What is God wanting me to do? Don't start with the 'How' question. If God gives you the 'What,' then God can show you the 'How.'" Who holds the pen in your life?

The story of Joseph is not really about the dream of Joseph. The story of Joseph is about the dream of God.

God is the source of the dream. God is the giver of the dream. God has a dream for the world, and God had a dream for Joseph to make a difference in the world. God wanted him to make a big impact. The dream of God became the dream of Joseph. Joseph lived out that dream. What could be better than that? Like Joseph, we can be who God intends for us to be and do what God means for us to do. Take the blank page, hand God the pen, and ask Him to fill in the page any way He wants.

 # Find some quiet time with God.

That's not always an easy thing to do. Life is noisy.
There are lots of noises coming at us all of the time.

The Environmental Protection Agency
says 183,000,000 Americans live with excessive noise levels in their life.

We have the noise of television, the noise of the radio, the noise of the cell phone, and the noise of the Internet coming at us all of the time, screaming for our attention.

In the middle of the noise, it can be hard to hear what is going on in your own heart.

➣ *what happened to me* ➢

I recently attended a football game, and I had my cell phone with me because I was expecting an important call from a friend. People were screaming and the music was blaring. There was so much noise around me that when my friend finally called me, I didn't hear my phone ring. I missed the call because of all the noise. We live in a noisy world. God may be trying to call us to drop a dream in our hearts, but we can't hear the phone because there's too much noise going on around us.

What if you turned off the noise and spent some quiet time before God?

It may be a quiet place in your backyard, at the beach, your favorite park, or in a chapel. Find a quiet place where you can have some alone time with Him. Quiet yourself before Him. Listen to what is going on in your heart.

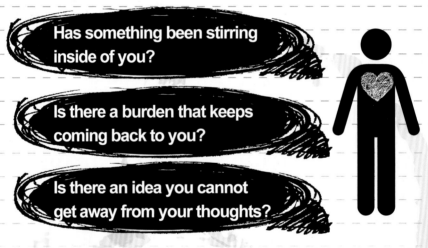

Has something been stirring inside of you?

Is there a burden that keeps coming back to you?

Is there an idea you cannot get away from your thoughts?

This is one of the ways God speaks to us.

When our son, Blake, was two years old, we took him to Disneyland. While we were in line to ride Dumbo, I was holding him in my arms. All at once he took hold of my cheeks with both of his hands and moved my face to establish eye contact with me. He wanted to make sure that he had my full attention. Sometimes I think God would like to take hold of our cheeks and make sure He has our full attention.

The Bible says, "Find a quiet, secluded place...and you will begin to sense His grace" **(Matthew 6:6 MSG)**.

It seems that even in our quiet time with God, we can find it hard to be quiet before Him. When I spend time alone with Him, I usually do a lot of talking. I tell Him this and I tell Him that. What I have to say to Him may be important, but what He has to say to me is even more important.

Sometimes I just need to put my hand over my mouth so I can hear what is going on in my heart and learn to hear His voice.

God wants to drop a dream in our hearts. We just have to be quiet enough to hear it.

I heard about a mom who was said to have the gift of gab. She could talk and talk a million miles a minute. One day she took her little boy in the car with her and she was talking the whole time, saying this, and saying that. Finally, she said, "We need to go by the store and get some buttons." Her little boy looked up at her and said, "Mom, you need a button for your mouth."

Sometimes I need a button for my mouth. I need to quiet my spirit, quiet my soul, and put a button on my mouth so I can hear what is going on in my heart. God may be trying to drop a dream in my heart but there is so much noise that I cannot hear it.

The Bible says, "Be still, and know that I am God" **(Psalm 46:10)**.

Maybe that's why God dropped the dream in Joseph's heart in his sleep. I can't be sure about that, but I do know when you are sleeping you are pretty still. When you're sleeping, you're not busy doing this or that. When you're sleeping there isn't noise coming from here or noise coming from there.

When we learn to be still and listen to what is going on in our heart, God can speak to us and drop His God-sized dream into our hearts.

Check out the way you are wired by God.

If you really want this point to stick with you, put the book down and look for a pair of shoes in the house that are not your shoes. Put those shoes on. Find a pair of shoes that are too small for you or find a pair of shoes that are too big for you. Take off your shoes and put on those other shoes. Doesn't that feel uncomfortable?

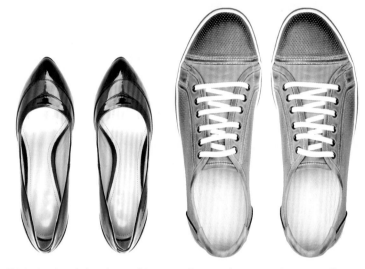

Pick the book back up. Now, you're ready to continue reading. We all know the importance of wearing a pair of shoes that are the right fit for you. If you walk around with shoes that are too small for you, or shoes that are too big for you, you end up with blisters on your feet or you might trip and fall.

You want to put on a pair of shoes that are the right fit for you.

The same thing is true when it comes to a dream. You want to take hold of a dream that is the right fit for the way God made you. When God made you, He made you the way He did so you could fulfill the dream He has for your life. He has given you the gifts and the talents you have. He has given you the passion and the strengths you have. He has given you the personality you have.

The Bible says, "You created my inmost being. You knit me together in my mother's womb" **(Psalm 139:13).**

You are not here by accident. You are not here by chance. God made you the way He did so you could fulfill the dream He has for your life.

I had dinner with a professional football player, **Jon Ritchie,** who played the position of fullback. He was a big guy with muscles on his muscles. His arms were bigger than my legs. His forehead was shaped like a battering ram. He looked like he could run through a steel wall. During dinner he looked at me with this big grin on his face and said, "When God made me He made me to be a fullback." It seems to me he was right. I am not wired to be a fullback. If I tried to be a fullback, I would end up on my back in some hospital. But this guy, he looked like a fullback, he was built like a fullback; he ate like a fullback (I know, because I picked up the tab for dinner); and he was wired to be a fullback.

The same idea is true for you. When God made you, He made you the way He made you so you could fulfill the dream He has for your life.

GIFT OF LEADERSHIP   **BEING A RULER**

When we look at the life of Joseph, he had been given the gift of leadership. That gift was on the inside of him; it just had to be discovered, and deployed. God is the one who gave him that gift. Then God gave him a dream of being a ruler that was the right fit for the way he was made.

His dream was linked to the way he was wired.

DISCOVER → DEVELOP → DEPLOY

God gave you a footprint. His dream for you is the right match for that footprint.

What are your **strengths** and how could God use them?

What are your **talents** and how could God use them?

What are the **gifts** God has given you and how could God use them?

How could God use the **passion** He has given you?

How could God use the **personality** He has given you?

Discover what you have. Develop what you have. Deploy what you have. God gave you a footprint and His dream for you is the right match for that footprint. The way the shoe fits is one of the clues to finding the dream He has for your life.

I now pastor the church my dad had pastored since 1965. Early in my own ministry, sometimes I was asked how in the world I was going to fill his shoes. He was such a great pastor. He had very big shoes. If I tried to fill his shoes I would have ended up with blisters on my feet. I came to the point where I realized I did not have to try to fit in his shoes.

I just had to wear the shoes God had given me and then I could fulfill the dream God had for me.

My dad & me

I hope you will do the same. In fact, this may be a good place to take off those shoes that do not fit and put your own shoes back on. Doesn't that feel a whole lot better?

There are many ways and many places where God can drop a dream in your heart. When you surrender your life to God, find a way to spend some quiet time with Him, and check out the way He wired you, you have put yourself in position to find and follow your God-sized dream.

The Bible says, "Trust God from the bottom of your heart; do not try to figure out everything on your own. Listen for the voice of God in everything you do, and everywhere you go, He is the one keeping you on track" **(Proverbs 3:5-6 MSG).**

Navigation System

1. God isn't looking for us to bring our dreams to Him so He can bless them. He wants to give us His dreams. Take a few moments to quiet yourself and ask Him to show you what His dream is for you. Picture yourself handing the pen over to God and letting Him write His dream for you. Write out any thoughts that He gives you:

2. Take a moment to reflect on your life and ask God to show you moments when you were experiencing His pleasure as you carried out a responsibility, fulfilled an obligation, touched someone's life, or made a difference in some way. Create a list of your talents, strengths and passions:

TALENTS

PASSIONS

STRENGTHS

3. The Bible says, "Offer yourself as a living sacrifice to God, dedicated to His service. Let God transform you, then you will be able to know the will of God, what is good, pleasing and perfect" (Romans 12:1-2 GNT). Even though you may have already done this at some point in your history, the word "offer" is in the present continuous tense, implying it is an ongoing choice we are to make. Take a moment to turn that verse into a prayer:

4. Pray this prayer: *Lord, I offer myself as a living sacrifice to You, dedicated to Your service. Transform me, so I will be able to know Your will, what is good pleasing and perfect for my life. Amen.*

Write a prayer asking God to help you surrender to Him so you may hear what His dream is for you:

chapter**FOUR**

chapter ONE
chapter TWO
chapter THREE
chapter FOUR

Firm Grip

"To infinity and beyond!"
— Buzz Lightyear in *Toy Story*

a story I heard

There was a high school senior who was asked to write a paper on what he wanted to be when he grew up. He wrote about his dream of someday owning a horse ranch. The teacher gave him an 'F' on his paper and said, "This is an unrealistic dream for you. You have no money. You have no resources. There is no way you could ever do it. If you rewrite this paper with a more realistic goal, I will reconsider your grade."

The boy thought it over for a week and then turned in the paper with no changes at all. He said, *"You keep the 'F', and I'll keep my dream!"*

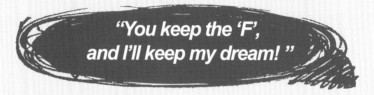

"You keep the 'F', and I'll keep my dream! "

The boy held onto his dream and one day that dream became a reality. He did own a horse ranch. Years later, the same teacher who had encouraged him to give up on his dream apologized to him and said, "When I was a teacher I stole a lot of kids' dreams. Fortunately, you had enough gumption to protect your dream."

When you have a dream, keep a firm grip on that dream and let that dream keep a firm grip on you.

DRE^AM STEALER

 ## Refuse to let anyone change or steal your dream

Stacy Allison was the first American woman ever to climb Mt. Everest. That's not an easy thing to do. Looking back on her experience, she said something I thought was interesting. "Sometimes in your life, it's OK not to listen to what other people are saying," she said. "If I had listened to other people, I would not have climbed." Refuse to let others take away your dream.

You know where you're headed, you know where you're going, and you're on your way to reaching your dream. There will be those who do not believe in your dream. They will not be crazy about that dream. They will criticize you and your dream. They will try to discourage you and laugh at your dream. They will give you a list of reasons why it could never happen.

If you let them, they will rip that dream right out of your hands. Moments in life arise when you have to stop listening to the words of others—words that create discouragement, words that create despair, and words that cause you to give up on your dream.

Refuse to let others take away your dream.

I heard about one lady whose husband was in the hospital. When she checked in at the nurse's station, she asked how her husband was doing. The nurse said, "Your husband is in critical condition." The lady was shocked. She had just seen her husband the day before and he had seemed to be doing better. She asked the nurse about it again, "Are you sure it is my husband you are talking about?" The nurse said, "Yes, it is your husband. He is in critical condition. He is critical of the doctors, critical of the nurses, critical of the room, and critical of the food. Your husband is in critical condition."

When you have a dream in your heart you are going to run into those who are in critical condition. They will criticize you and your dream.

Refuse to let others take away your dream.

In the story of Joseph, his brothers were critical of him and his dream. They weren't crazy about their brother to begin with, and when he told them his dream:

"They hated him even more because of his dream" **(Genesis 37:8).**

When he told them about his dream of being a leader, they were not happy or excited for their brother. They did not ask their brother what they could do to help him on his way to his dream. Instead, they had a very negative reaction to their brother and his dream.

Just like Joseph, you must have a firm grip on your dream and your dream must have a firm grip on you.

"Don't let the noise of others' opinions drown out your own inner voice."

— Steve Jobs
Founder of Apple Inc.

48

Keep your eyes on the God who is for you. This will help you keep a grip on your dream.

The more you focus on **your critics** and think about your critics, the bigger and stronger your critics will seem to be. It will seem like they can rip your dream right out of your hands.

The more you focus on **God** and think about Him, the smaller and less powerful your critics will seem. God is much bigger and much stronger than your critics.

If His hands are around your hands, no one will ever rip your dream out of your hands.

"If God is for us who can be against us?" **(Romans 8:31)**.

If God is with you and God is for you, it doesn't matter who or what is against you. If God put a dream in your heart, He has the power to bring it to pass. The only one who really has the power to keep that dream from happening is you. If you are feeling discouraged, let Him wrap His hands around your hands and firm up the grip you have on your dream. You're not living for your critics, you're living for Him.

Keep your eyes on the dream in front of you. This will help you keep a grip on your dream.

My niece, Katie, is 11 years old. One day she told my brother she is going to go to Stanford University. My brother didn't go to Stanford. He is smarter than me, but he is not that smart. She has it in her heart to go to Stanford so she put up a picture of Stanford in her room and she keeps that dream in a place where she can see it. I do not know where she got the idea, (I am pretty sure she didn't get it from my brother), but it's a good idea.

Write out your dream.
Keep that dream in a place where you can see it.

Many places exist where you can post your dream so you see it often: on your bathroom mirror, on the fridge, on the dashboard of your car, on your computer screen, or staple it to your forehead. As you work toward your dream, keep the dream in a place where you can see it. See yourself moving toward and reaching your dream. See the benefits and the joy of reaching your dream.

"Jesus never lost sight of where He was headed. He could put up with anything along the way" **(Hebrews 12:2 MSG)**.

Keep that dream where you can see it and it will help you keep your grip.

Keep your eyes on the dream team around you.

Anytime you have a dream, there will be those who do not believe in you and do not believe in your dream. You cannot do much about that. What you can do is build your own dream team. Find people who do believe in you and in your dream. Ask them to pray for you, stand with you, and believe with you as you follow your dream. Share your heart with them. Spend time with them. Let them speak into your life and your dream. That dream team can help you to keep your grip.

I have a dream to have 20 church sites around the San Francisco Bay Area. It is a dream God has dropped in my heart. We want to reach more people with the love of Jesus and let them know how much they matter to God. As of this printing, we are halfway toward reaching this dream. God has built an amazing dream team around me who help me keep my grip.

One weekend when we were getting ready to launch some new sites, I found myself nervous and anxious as I fought against doubt and fear. It felt like I was losing my grip. Then I received a text from a friend who is a part of my dream team. He lives on the other side of the country. He did not know the struggle I was having at that moment, but he sent me a text that said,

When I read those words, faith began to rise in my heart. My hands were strong. That is what happens when you build a dream team around you and your dream.

"Two are better than one" **(Ecclesiastes 4:9).**

A dream team can help you keep your grip.

 # It's About More than Just You

Take hold of the dream and let that dream take hold of you.

Do not let anyone rip that dream out of your hand. The dream is about you, but it is about more than just you. The dream Joseph had about being a leader was about him, but it was about much more than just him. As we follow his story we're going to see that when his dream came to pass, he was in a leadership position in the right place at the right time. Because of his leadership, he would save the lives of thousands of others. Joseph's dream ends up putting him in position to save an African nation from famine.

That's why the dream that you have matters so much.

It is about you, but it is about more than just you.

You may not see it now, you may not know it now, but when your dream comes to pass it may touch the world in ways that only God knows.

Roma's Story

We had a special guest with us during a Christmas message series, Roma Downey, star of the CBS hit television show, *Touched by an Angel*. Roma is a talented actress, singer, and producer who really made her mark in the role of the angel on that program.

Now, she's married to Mark Burnett, one of the most successful television producers in Hollywood. They are working on exciting projects together that honor God. They just produced an incredibly successful mini-series titled *The Bible.* But how does something like that happen — Roma becoming a successful actress and producer in Hollywood?

It started with a dream.

ROMA DOWNEY, MY WIFE ALISA, AND ME

"I had a dream, from the time I was a little girl growing up in Ireland," she said. Roma was raised in war-torn Northern Ireland, and eventually made her way "across the pond," to New York City to try her hand at acting. She had a God-sized dream to be successful in show business in America. "I had an opportunity to go in and read for an Irish Spring soap commercial," she recalled. "I was sure because I was Irish that I was a shoe-in." She eagerly awaited the call telling her she got the job, but her agent finally informed her, "You didn't get the part. Apparently you didn't sound Irish enough." Roma pressed on, not letting go of her dream.

She shared with our congregation how one of her very first jobs in New York City was as a coat-check girl in a fancy restaurant on the Upper West Side. One of the first coats she ever checked was that of TV personality Regis Philbin.

"He checked his coat with me, and I was kind of dreamily looking out, imagining what it would be like to one day be a customer in a restaurant like this," she said. "When Regis came back to get his coat, we got into a conversation, and he left me a really generous tip. Well, only in America… three or four years later, I was now starring in *Touched By An Angel*. I was invited back to New York City to be the guest star on — you guessed it — the *Regis Philbin Show*," she said.

"Dreams can come true."

When God drops a God-sized dream in your heart, it's bigger than just you. Roma soon learned that God would use *Touched By An Angel* to change lives forever.

"We had one young lady that came up to me at an event. She had very fresh scars on her wrists. Clearly she had tried to take her own life. She shared that she was very angry and felt very abandoned by her family and God. She felt utterly alone and had decided to take her own life. As she cut her wrists, she slid down the wall in the bathroom ready to die. In her bedroom, coincidentally, she'd left the television on. And coincidentally, *Touched by an Angel* was on and the scene that was playing was the Angel Revelation scene when I was speaking to someone on the show and said, 'You know what? You are not alone. And you have never been alone, because God loves you.' This young lady heard those words in her own darkness. It spoke right to her heart."

Roma went on to say the woman called an ambulance and asked for help, and gave her life to God in that moment. "We were just a TV show," she said. "But I really believe God was working through all of us to bring His message."

Your dream is about you, but it's not about just you. Ask Roma Downey.

SCAN: The interview with Roma Downey is available through this QR code or go to www.cathedraloffaith.org/romadowney

 *reflection*

Firm Grip

1. As you read through each chapter of this book, I am praying God's dream
   for you will become clearer. In this space, write out what God is revealing to
   you right now:

   ----

2. Decide the best place you could put your dream image so it will be in front
   of you. You might write it or type it and place it in your Bible, on your mirror,
   next to your desk, or on your screen saver. Until God makes your dream
   completely clear, write out a prayer asking Him to show you His dream, and
   then put it in one of those places.

3. Identify one or two people who would be supportive of you on your dream journey. Take time to sit with them and share your dream. Let them know how they can be praying for you and how they can best give you their support. Write their names here:

4. Here's my prayer for you, as you read this book. Read it prayerfully in agreement with me: *"God, You are starting to stir things up in the hearts of those who are reading this book. You are stirring them to believe again. May those who are reading this book, sense Your work in them. Unfold Your dream and Your purpose before them, and drop something into their hearts that they can take hold of—something from You. Let Your dream become their dream and help them begin to imagine living that dream. Thank You for what You are doing and for what You are going to do as You release Your dreams in them. Amen."*

section II

Section 2: Pit Stop

"So it came about when Joseph came to his brothers, that they stripped Joseph of his robe… and they took him and threw him into the pit" (Genesis 37:23-24 NASB).

chapter FIVE

Black Hole

"I knew if I could just get out of the first pit stop in the lead, we would have a chance."
— Justin Wilson, Race Car Driver

chapter SIX
chapter SEVEN
chapter EIGHT

One lady at our church, Thuy, had a dream to go back to college. To some that might not seem like a big deal, but for her it seemed like the impossible dream. She moved to this country when she was 17 years old, and then went through a divorce when she was 25. She was left to support her two children all by herself. It seemed like the dream of going to college had died, but God brought it back to life. She went back to college and graduated from San Jose State University. She said that her children were so proud of her that on the way home from the graduation ceremony they rolled down the car windows and screamed at the top of their lungs,

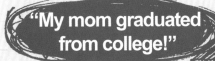

"My mom graduated from college!"

Thuy said, "I thank Jesus for His love because His love has created an amazing work in me!"

When you have a dream God drops in your heart, it may be a dream to ...

GO BACK TO COLLEGE

START YOUR OWN BUSINESS

HAVE A BETTER MARRIAGE

OWN YOUR OWN HOME

BREAK A BAD HABIT

WORK WITH AT-RISK KIDS

When you have a God-sized dream and you start to follow the dream, on the way to your dream, you may end up facing a pit stop. No one wants to be in the pit. No one likes to be in a pit. No one plans to be in a pit. But life just works out that way sometimes.

Humorist **Erma Bombeck** wrote, "If life is a bowl of cherries then what am I doing in the pits?"

Life is not always a bowl of cherries—sometimes it is the pits.

Jesus said, "In this world you will have trouble." It doesn't say you may have trouble or you could have trouble in this world. You will have trouble… but then He adds, "Take heart, for I have overcome the world" **(John 16:33).**

On the way to your God-sized dream, you may end up making a pit stop. That's what happened to Joseph.

In Genesis 37, we read about this part of his journey. He has a God-sized dream of becoming a leader and on the way to his dream he literally ends up in a pit. It is a case of sibling rivalry that goes really bad. In most every family there is a little bit of sibling rivalry.

SIBLING RIVALRY ➡

I heard a story about one six-year-old girl who came home from a Girl Scout meeting and proudly told her dad, "I am officially a Brownie." Not to be outdone, her three-year-old brother proudly announced, "I am a cupcake."

Sibling rivalry starts out when we are very young and most every family has their share of it. But if you throw envy into the mix and if you throw jealousy into the mix, that's when it can get ugly. That is what happened to Joseph.

A bad case of sibling rivalry landed Joseph in the pit.

His father, Jacob, made the mistake of fanning the flames of sibling rivalry. Experts warn parents about the mistake of playing favorites. You would think Jacob would have been the last one to make this mistake, because he had seen first-hand the problems it can cause. His own parents had made the mistake of playing favorites and it led to all kinds of trouble between his brother and him. But instead of learning from their mistake, he repeated their mistake and played favorites in his family. Joseph was his favorite son. He treated Joseph as his favorite son. He gave Joseph a special coat of many colors to wear because he was his favorite son.

Jacob made the mistake of **fanning the flames of sibling rivalry.**

Joseph himself made the mistake of fanning the flames of sibling rivalry. He played the part of the favorite son. One day he went out into the field to see his brothers and he was wearing that special coat that his dad had given him. This was not the kind of coat you would wear out in the field. It was the kind of coat that you might wear to a church service or to a nice dinner, but it was not the kind of coat that you would wear in the fields. When Joseph went to see his brothers in the field wearing this coat, he was strutting his stuff. He knew he was the favorite, they knew he was the favorite. He didn't have to work out in the field—all he had to do was strut his stuff around the field. Joseph himself made the mistake of fanning the flames of sibling rivalry.

Envy gets thrown into the mix.

Jealousy gets thrown into the mix. That's when it gets ugly. When Joseph came out to the fields to see his brothers, they decided this was their chance. They were so full of envy and jealousy. They wanted to get rid of this dreamer and all his dreams once and for all. They took their own flesh and blood, tore off the special coat he was wearing, and threw him into an empty well. Joseph ended up at the bottom of the pit. He had a dream in his heart, but on the way to the dream he ends up at the bottom of a pit.

It looked like this was the end of the dreamer and his dream.

Even as you read these words, you may be stuck in the bottom of a pit.

You have a dream in your heart but on your way to your dream you ended up in a pit. Someone may have put you in the pit. You may have put yourself in the pit. At this point, it doesn't matter how you got there. You just know you're in the pit, and when you're in the bottom of the pit, you can feel like this is the end of the dreamer and his dream. What you do when you're in the pit can determine whether it becomes a pit stop or whether it becomes a pit stay. It's one thing for you to have a pit stop—it's another thing to have a pit stay.

In this world you will have trouble, but with God's help, you can overcome. You can overcome every pit life throws at you. You may have a pit stop, but it doesn't have to be a pit stay.

Back in 1978, a young man ran into a pit. While working at the local hardware store, he was fired from his job. When you're fired from a job, that's the pits. But instead of it turning into a pit stay, he turned it into just a pit stop. He decided he would use the situation as an opportunity to start his own business. He found a business partner, and together they opened their own hardware store. They opened that first hardware store in 1979, and today they have over two thousand stores worldwide. The name of that young man was Bernard Marcus, and the name of the store he opened was

The Home Depot.

What you do when you run into a pit can turn it from a pit stay to just a pit stop — just a pit stop on the way to your dream.

Black Hole

1. What are some of the thoughts and emotions Joseph might have had when he was thrown in the pit?

2. Jesus said, "In this world you will have trouble. Take heart, for I have overcome the world"(John 16:33). How can this scripture be an encouragement to you the next time you end up in a pit?

3. Join me in praying this prayer: *Lord, help me to see where I am in my journey from Your perspective. I may be in the middle of a chapter and I can't figure out how it ends. But You, Lord, know how all of this works out. Give me Your peace and strength as I anticipate what You have prepared for me. Amen.*

chapter SIX ➜

chapter FIVE

chapter SIX

Power
in the Pit

"A pessimist sees the difficulty in every opportunity; an optimist sees the opportunity in every difficulty."

— Sir Winston Churchill
Former Prime Minister of Great Britain

chapter SEVEN
chapter EIGHT

A mom and dad were worried that their twin boys' personalities were quite extreme — one a pessimist, one an optimist. The parents took the boys to a psychiatrist, who began treating the pessimist. Trying to brighten his outlook, the psychiatrist took him to a room piled high with new toys. Instead of screaming with joy, the little boy burst into tears. "What's the matter?" the psychiatrist asked, baffled. "Don't you want to play with any of the toys?" "Yes," the little boy bawled, "but if I did I'd only break them."

Next he worked with the optimist. Trying to dampen his outlook, he took him to a room piled to the ceiling with horse manure. But instead of wrinkling his nose in disgust, the optimist gave a yelp of delight. He climbed to the top of the pile, dropped to his knees, and began gleefully digging out scoop after scoop with his bare hands. "What do you think you're doing?" the psychiatrist asked, baffled. "With all this manure," the little boy answered, beaming,

"There must be a pony in here somewhere!"

The pit can turn you into a bitter person, or the pit can turn you into a better person. It all depends on your attitude.

You can't always control what happens in your life, but when you find yourself in the bottom of the pit, you still have the power to choose. You can choose how you will respond to the pit. You aren't powerless while you're in the pit. If you think you're powerless, you'll feel helpless and hopeless. Remember, you have the power to choose how you will respond.

POWER

This may be the most important power of all.

One football coach, **Lou Holtz**, said, "Ten percent of life is what happens to you and ninety percent of life is how you respond to what happens to you."

The power to choose the attitude you have, the power to choose the response you have — this may be the most important power of all. Don't surrender your power to the pit. It may seem that the pit has the power to control you. It only has the power to control you if you give it that power.

You can take back your power from the pit. You don't have the power to control everything that happens around you or everything that happens to you, but you are not powerless.

Viktor Frankl, a renowned psychiatrist, was a prisoner in the concentration camps of World War II. It was the worst kind of pit possible. The pit had taken virtually everything away from him, but there was one thing he would not surrender to the pit. He would not surrender his power to the pit.

He put it this way, "The one thing you can't take away from me is the way I choose to respond to what you do to me. The last of one's freedoms is to choose one's attitude in any given circumstance."

The pit can turn you into a bitter person, or the pit can turn you into a better person.

It all depends on what you do with it and how you respond to it.

Better

POWER

Bitter

When you are in the pit, don't surrender your power to the pit. You have the power to choose how you respond to the pit.

As a pastor, I've seen many people face pits in their life and here is one thing I've discovered. You can put two people in the very same pit, with the very same problems, with the very same troubles, with the very same adversity, and one of them will come out of the pit bitter, and one of them will come out of the pit better. It's not the pit that makes the difference. It's how you respond to the pit that determines the outcome. This is the power you have. You can curl up in the corner of the pit and become negative, cynical, and bitter. Or you can say,

> **"With the help of God, this pit is not going to make me bitter, instead this pit is going to make me a better person."**

One thing we'll discover about Joseph is his time in the pit didn't turn him into a bitter person. As a matter of fact, his time in the pit was just the first of a series of problems he would face on his journey toward seeing his God-sized dream manifested in his life. But the pit and the problems didn't turn him into a bitter person. Each problem he encountered turned him into a better person.

The problems we face don't make us bitter or better. It is how we respond to the problems that make us bitter or better. Circumstances never make us feel or act or think a certain way unless we surrender our power to them. We have the power to choose how we think and how we act. How we think and act will ultimately influence how we feel about our problems. We are responsible for our responses.

On your way to your dream when you find yourself in a pit, don't surrender your power to the pit. Take back your power and refuse to get bitter—choose to become better.

Even while you're at the bottom of that pit,

1. CHOOSE JOY OVER DEPRESSION AND HOPE OVER DESPAIR.

2. TRUST GOD FOR STRENGTH AND THE NEXT STEPS YOU NEED TO TAKE.

3. FORGIVE OTHERS INSTEAD OF BLAMING THEM FOR WHERE YOU ARE.

4. CHOOSE CONFIDENCE OVER FEEL-INGS OF FEAR, UNCERTAINTY AND INSECURITY.

5. MAKE THE BEST OF THE BAD SITUATION.

6. KEEP BELIEVING IN THE DREAM YOU HAVE IN YOUR HEART.

7. DON'T SURRENDER YOUR POWER TO THE PIT. TAKE BACK YOUR POWER.

8. REFUSE TO BECOME BITTER. CHOOSE TO BECOME BETTER.

Say it out loud one more time,

"I choose to be better, not bitter."

⋙ *Bethany Hamilton* ⋘

That is what one young lady named Bethany Hamilton decided to do. She was born into a family of surfers, began surfing at a young age and had a God-sized dream to one day become a professional surfer. But on the way to her dream she found herself in the bottom of a pit. At the age of 13 while surfing in Hawaii, a 15-foot tiger shark attacked Bethany. Even though she lost 60 percent of her blood, she miraculously survived the attack.

BETHANY HAMILTON

But she lost her left arm in the attack and it looked like her dream was over. It would have been easy for her to become bitter, bitter about the attack, bitter about losing her arm. Instead of becoming bitter, she chose to become better. She couldn't change what had happened to her and the tragedy of losing her arm. What she could choose was how she would respond.

She decided not to give up on her dream. She got back in the water and learned how to surf with the one arm she had. Bethany continued to surf, to compete, and even win. In 2007, the dream she had in her heart became reality and she turned pro. She still competes with the best surfers in the world. Bethany has shared her life story in her autobiography, *Soul Surfer*, which has been turned into a movie. She has been able to share how her faith helped her every step of the way. Her life has been an inspiration to people all over the world. "I could never have embraced this many people with two arms," she wrote in her book.

It's not what happens to you. It's how you respond to what happens to you that matters most. On the way to your dream, when you fall into the pit, do not surrender your power to the pit.

"You can do all things through Him who gives you strength" **(Philippians 4:13)**.

Do not become bitter—choose to become better.

Power in the Pit

1. One of the ways we prolong our pit stops is by only focusing on the person or circumstances that put us there. Ask God to help you to forgive yourself, or someone else, focusing on God, rather than how you got in the pit. Write out below anything God is saying to you about this.

2. The difference between *better* and *bitter* is the letter, "I." If "I" can't get out of the way "I" will end up bitter. What choices do you need to make in order to end up better?

3. Pray with me: *Lord, help me to realize You give me a choice when I end up in a pit. Help me remember that I am not always responsible for the circumstances that I am in, but I am responsible for the way that I allow them to affect me. They can get on top of me or they can transform me in what You want me to be. Make me more like You. Amen.*

chapter SEVEN ➡

- chapter FIVE
- chapter SIX

- chapter **SEVEN**

Extreme Makeover

"What doesn't kill you makes you stronger."

— Kelly Clarkson, First *American Idol* Winner

- chapter EIGHT

On the way to your dream, you're going to run into a pit.

DREAM

Mother Teresa once said this about being in the pit, "I know God won't give me anything I can't handle, I just wish He didn't trust me so much."

On the way to your dream, you're going to run into a pit.

You do not have to look for the pit, the pit has a way of looking for you. You never come out of the pit the same way you go into it. You'll come out of the pit as a bitter person or you'll come out of the pit as a better person. It all depends on how you choose to respond. When you're in the pit, you can choose to change the way you view the pit. You may not like it, you may not want to be in it, but you can change the way you view the pit.

If you give the pit an extreme makeover, the pit will give you an extreme makeover in the best kind of way.

TURN THE PIT INTO A CLASSROOM

Give the pit an extreme makeover!

Hang up a chalkboard, pull up a desk, take out your notebook, and pull out your pen. Give the pit an extreme makeover.

**A classroom is a place of learning.
There are lessons you can learn from the pit.
There are lessons about God,
about yourself, and about life.**

Some of the most important lessons you will learn are the lessons you learn from the school of hard knocks. In one *Peanuts* comic, Linus says, "You know, Charlie Brown, they say we learn more from losing than from winning." Charlie Brown responds, "Then that must make me the smartest person in the world."

*Losing is the pits, and yet, some lessons
can only be learned from the pits.
You won't learn them anywhere else.*

TURN THE PIT
INTO A CLASSROOM

What is the lesson you can learn from the pit?

The Bible says that Jesus himself "learned obedience through the things that He suffered" **(Hebrews 5:8).**

Underline the word *learned*. Circle the word *learned*. Highlight the word *learned*. Understand some things can only be learned through suffering. It is not that you want to suffer, or you like to suffer, but there are some lessons you can only learn through suffering. What is the lesson you can learn from the pit?

Never waste a pain. Do not just put up with the pain. Make the pain useful. Never waste a pain. Instead take the painful pits of life and turn them into teaching moments for you—character building moments.

Oprah Winfrey
put it this way, "Turn your wounds into wisdom."

Some of the most important lessons you'll ever learn are those you learn when you're in the pit.

TURN THE PIT
INTO A CLASSROOM

There was a writer for *Newsweek* magazine who was in the pit. She was in a money pit. That is a tough pit in which to be. When you and your family fall into a money pit, it's a tough pit. This writer and her family fell into the money pit and they ended up losing their home. But even though losing your home is a painful pit, she wrote, "The loss of our home taught our family a valuable lesson. We learned that material possessions do not make you happy. In fact, for every material thing that we lost, we gained something of greater value."

On the way to your God-sized dream when you fall into a pit, give the pit an extreme makeover. In the best kind of way, it will give you an extreme makeover, and you'll leave the pit with the wisdom you need as you're on your way to your dream.

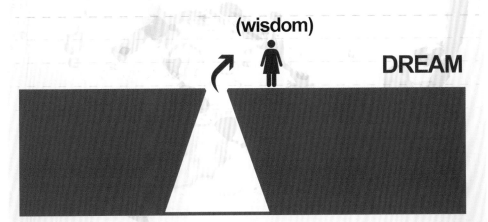

(wisdom)

DREAM

TURN THE PIT INTO THE CLEANERS

Get out an iron and an ironing board. Allow God to use the pit to get the wrinkles out of your character.

Turn the pit into the cleaners.

Look at the picture of the two shirts below.

1.

2.

Notice the first shirt is all wrinkled. There are wrinkles in the front, and wrinkles in the back. There are wrinkles on the sides and wrinkles in the arms and around the collar. The second shirt is different. There are no wrinkles in this shirt. All of the wrinkles are gone. The reason there are no wrinkles in this second shirt is it has felt the pressure and the heat of the iron. The pressure and the heat eliminated the wrinkles.

When you walk through the pressure and the heat of a difficult situation, you can choose to let that trial iron out the wrinkles in your character.

TURN THE PIT
INTO THE CLEANERS

The Bible tells us heat and pressure develop our character.

"We can rejoice, too, when we run into problems and trials, for we know that they help us develop endurance. And endurance develops strength of character" **(Romans 5:3-4 NLT).**

When you feel the pressure of the pit and things are heating up, this will remove some of those wrinkles from your character and develop the endurance and the strength you need on your way to your dream. This is reason you can rejoice when you are in the pit. You don't rejoice because you're in the pit, you rejoice because of what the pit will do for you. You rejoice that God will use that pit to grow you, mature you, and get the wrinkles out of your character.

God is more concerned about your character than He is your comfort. You can use the heat and the pressure of the pit to get rid of the wrinkles in your character. Even though you're in the pit, don't let the pit get into you.

This is how you thrive in the pit. You don't just have to survive the pit, instead you can learn to thrive in the pit.

Take the pit and turn it into a classroom.

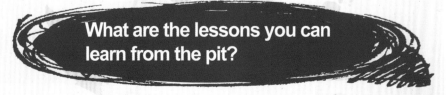

What are the lessons you can learn from the pit?

Take the pit and turn it into the cleaners.

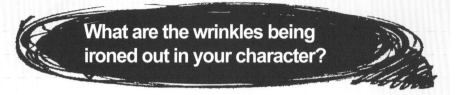

What are the wrinkles being ironed out in your character?

You don't have to look for the pit; you don't have to like the pit. Being in the pit is the pits—that is why it is called the pits. But, on the way to your dream when the pit shows up, you can do more than survive the pit. You can learn to thrive in the pit. When you give the pit an extreme makeover, then the pit will give you an extreme makeover in the best kind of way.

You will leave the pit a much wiser person. You will leave the pit a much deeper person. You'll leave the pit much more prepared to take hold of the dream God has for your life.

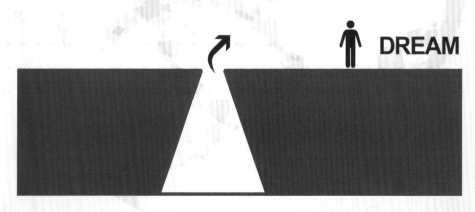

DREAM

Extreme Makeover

1. Think about the last time you faced adversity. Write out one of the lessons you took away from it.

2. God is building character in you. Which of the following traits is He working on in you at this time?

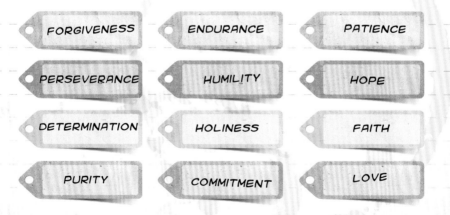

FORGIVENESS ENDURANCE PATIENCE

PERSEVERANCE HUMILITY HOPE

DETERMINATION HOLINESS FAITH

PURITY COMMITMENT LOVE

3. Take a moment to pray, *Lord, come and help me do a makeover in my life. As you redecorate my life, give me the strength to get rid of attitudes and thoughts that won't work in the new design. Have Your way in my life as You give new designs to replace my old outdated ways. Amen.*

chapterEIGHT ➡

chapter FIVE
chapter SIX
chapter SEVEN
chapter EIGHT

Exit Strategy

"We dreamers have our ways, of facing rainy days, and somehow we survive."

— Barry Manilow, *Award Winning Singer / Songwriter*

I once had a chance to visit one of the largest mazes in the world. On the outside of the maze, they tell you the average time it takes to get through it. When I walked into the maze, I went this way and ran into a dead end. I went that way and ran into a dead end. At that point you start to scratch your head. You wonder if you will find your way out of the maze. You wonder if there is a way out of the maze, but I knew there was a way out and so I kept on making my way through. Eventually, I made my way out of the maze. I am sure I did not break any records, but I did find my way out.

**That is what keeps you going —
you know there is a way into the maze and
there is a way out of the maze.**

When you're on your way to your dream and you find yourself in the bottom of a pit, it can feel like that maze. You look this way and all you can see is a dead end. You look that way and all you see is a dead end.

You start to scratch your head and wonder if there is a way out of the pit, and that's when you look up. You look up and you see God is still with you, God is still for you and God still has a dream for your life. He will make a way, when there seems to be no way out of the pit. He can make a way out of the pit. That is what keeps you going.

Hold onto your hope. If there is a way into a pit, there is a way out of the pit. You won't be in the pit forever— beyond the pit there is still the palace.

One of the greatest promises of Scripture tells us, "We know that God causes everything to work together for the good of those who love God and are called according to his purpose" **(Romans 8:28 NLT).**

It does not say everything that happens in your life is good. It does not say everything that happens in your life comes from God. There are plenty of things that happen that are not good, and there are plenty of things that happen in your life that are not from God.

What it does say is God is able to take everything that happens in your life, work it together for your good and for His glory. If there was a way into the pit, there is a way out of the pit. He will make a way out of the pit. Beyond the pit there is still a palace.

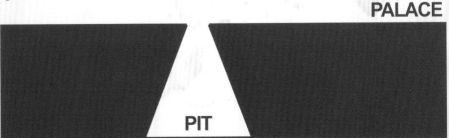

PALACE

PIT

One of the best examples of this is in the story of Joseph. Joseph goes from having a God-sized dream dropped into his heart to being dropped into a pit by his own brothers. As we walk through the maze with him, you'll see the pit was just the first of several bad things that happened. His brothers threw him into the pit, and then they turned around and sold him into slavery. If that isn't bad enough, he was then falsely accused of an immoral act and is unjustly thrown into prison in a foreign land. Then, he helps out a person while he is in the prison, but the person forgets to help him out. One bad thing after another happens on Joseph's journey toward his dream. It's as if he's stuck in a maze and runs into one dead end after another. And yet in the middle of all of these bad things, God was still at work to make sure that his dream would come to pass.

He says to his brothers, "You intended to harm me, but God intended it all for good" (Genesis 50:20 NLT).

This is an example of how God can use anything that happens to move us toward our divine destiny and fulfill the purpose He has for our lives.

God still makes a way where there seems to be no way, and beyond the pit there is still the palace.

If you're in the pit, don't give up on your dream.

During the filming of the movie *Ben Hur*, the lead actor, Charlton Heston, had trouble learning to drive a chariot. With a lot of practice he was finally able to control the chariot, but still had some doubts. He reportedly explained his concerns to the director saying, "I think I can drive the chariot, but I am not sure I can win the race."

The director replied,

"You just stay in the race and I will make sure you win."

When you find yourself in the pit and you wonder if you will ever make it out of the maze, keep the faith, hold onto your hope, and just stay in the race. God will make sure you win. He causes everything to work for your good and His glory. If there is a way into the pit there is a way out of the pit.

Beyond the pit, there is still the palace.
You are still on your way to your dream.

✑ *Ted Williams* ✑

You may be in a very deep pit. We had a guest at our church named Ted Williams. He had been in a very deep pit. You may remember him from YouTube. His story went viral with over 40,000,000 hits. He was homeless in Columbus, Ohio asking for money on the side of a road. He held a sign that said, "I have a God-given gift of voice." One day a local reporter stopped to give Ted some money and videotaped him speaking with that "golden voice." The reporter posted it on YouTube and millions of people got to know him and his story.

Ted had once been a successful radio announcer with a wife and a family, and then one day a friend gave him a cigarette laced with cocaine, and that was the start of his journey into a very deep pit.

He lost his job, he lost his home, he lost his family, and he lived with his addiction on the streets for many years. It was a very deep pit, but if there is a way into the pit, there is a way out of the pit. With the help of God, he has found his way.

Ted has gone through drug rehabilitation and at the writing of this book, has been clean and sober for almost three years. He has been able to reconnect with his family and repair relationships that were broken. Ted has been the voice on the Today Show, the voice of Super Bowl commercials, and is currently the voice of Kraft macaroni and cheese TV ads.

He is doing work to help others who are homeless and battling their addictions. He has recommitted his life to Christ, and Jesus is at work restoring his life, and recreating his dreams. The pit will not have the last word in his life.

God will have the last word in Ted's life.
God will have the last word in your life.
If there is a way into the pit,
there is a way out of the pit,
even a very deep pit.
Beyond the pit, there is still the palace.

SCAN: The interview with Ted William is available through this QR code or go to www.cathedraloffaith.org/tedwilliams

Exit Strategy

1. If you spend all of your time asking, "Y?", it will turn your P-I-T into P-I-T-"Y." Rather than "Why?" ask God "What?" He wants to do in your life. Write out anything He is saying to you.

2. God's promise is He will be with you wherever you go. How is this promise an encouragement to you when you find yourself in a pit?

3. Pray with me, *Lord, you specialize in making a way where there seems to be no way. I believe that You can work all things together for my good. Give me patience, infused with hope, as I await Your exit sign from this season. Help me overcome the feelings of loneliness in this pit, for I know that You are with me. Amen.*

section III ➡

Section 3: Desperate Housewife

"Joseph was well-built and handsome, and after a while his master's wife took notice of Joseph" (Genesis 39:6-7).

chapter NINE

On the
Job Training

"Dignify and glorify common labor. It is at the
bottom of life that we must begin, not at the top."
— Booker T. Washington, Educator and Author

chapter TEN
chapter ELEVEN
chapter TWELVE

I believe in miracles.

Any time I start to doubt miracles still happen, all I have to do is walk outside my office and over to the back parking lot. There are two basketball hoops in the back lot. Many people may look at those basketball hoops and that's all they see. But when I look at those basketball hoops, I see a miracle. When I first started to work at the church, putting up the basketball hoops was one my responsibilities. And now, 30 years later, those hoops are still standing. That's why I know miracles still happen. When I look back on my journey, it all started with doing jobs at the church like that. I would put up basketball hoops. I would edit the church newspaper. I would run the church lighting board. I was in charge of directing church traffic. I crawled under the stage to run special effects for the church drama. I taught classes for young adults in the hallways of the church.

I was not the best at what I did,
but I did the best with what I had.

In those early years of my journey, I learned an important lesson:

BLOOM WHERE YOU ARE PLANTED.

Do not wait until you have another job to do your very best. Do the very best with the job you have. Have a good attitude with the job you have. Develop your skills with the job you have. Work with a servant's heart with the job you have. Choose to be enthusiastic in the job you have. Find joy in the job you have. It may not be your dream job, but it's a job. You don't have to wait until you have another job to do your best. Do the very best that you can now. Putting up basketball hoops in the parking lot — that is where miracles happen.

Wherever you are,
make the most of your opportunity.
Bloom where you have been planted.

This is a phrase that was first used by a bishop in the sixteenth century, **St. Francis de Sales.** It means to make the most of wherever you are. If you are planted in a garden, then bloom there. If you are planted in a field, then bloom there. If you're planted in the middle of a bunch of weeds, then bloom there.

You don't have to wait until you're in a different place in order to bloom. You can make the best of a situation, even when you're in the weeds! Maybe you feel like you are in the weeds. There's a sign in one place of work that reads, *"This is not an office — this is hell with fluorescent lighting."*

If you feel like you're in the weeds—at work, at home, or at school—with the help of God, you can still find a way to shine. While you are on the way to your dream, decide to make the most of where you are.

Find a way to bloom
where you are planted.

We have been looking at a man in the Bible by the name of Joseph, and that's what we learn from his story. On the way to his God-sized dream, Joseph learned to bloom where he was planted. One night he had a *dream*, and that dream was of being a ruler. He ended up in the pit on the way to his dream. His brothers then sold him to a band of foreign traders. He ended up as a servant in another country at the house of a top military leader (Genesis 39:1).

At first, he worked outside of the house; then Joseph was promoted and he started working inside the house. While he was working inside the house, he received another promotion. He was put in charge of the entire estate. He was in charge of managing property, overseeing the staff, handling the finances — he had been put in charge of everything in the house and everything outside of the house.

EVERYTHING

staff & finances

managing property

in charge of the entire estate

working inside the house

working outside the house

PIT

The Scriptures don't tell us how long it took, but he was promoted all the way to the top. He had power, respect, authority, and privilege. Joseph made it all the way to the top because he bloomed where he was planted. He used his gifts and skills to the best of his ability at each job along the way. He did a good job with whatever he was given. It wasn't his dream job, but he didn't wait until he had his dream job to do a good job. Joseph turned each step into an opportunity to sharpen his skills as a leader. He was gifted as a leader, but his gifts still needed to be developed and fine-tuned.

His job at that time was preparing him for his future.

Do your best at whatever your work is today. Until you can be found faithful with little, you will not be promoted to more. Being faithful and fruitful today opens the door for your tomorrows.

Jesus put it this way, "Whoever can be trusted with little can also be trusted with much" **(Luke 16:10).**

There is a band called *Van Halen* that would make outrageous demands when they were touring. One demand was that in their dressing room there must be a bowl filled with M&Ms — but the bowl couldn't have any brown M&Ms in it. All of the brown M&M's had to be removed. When you hear of a request like that, it sounds kind of  crazy. It must be one of those weird rock-and-roll head games. But in his book, one of the leaders of the band wrote about the method behind the madness. He said whenever the band arrived and there was a bowl full of candy that lined up with their request, the more important issues were taken care of as well. When the bowl full of candy did not line up with their request, the more important issues were not taken care of either.

Band member *Dave Lee Roth* said if the M&M request wasn't met correctly, "We would line check the entire production and it was guaran-  teed we would run into trouble."

But if the "little" was taken care of, then the "much" would be taken care of, too.

Be faithful and fruitful with the little you have today, and it opens the door to your tomorrow.
Bloom where you are planted.

On the way to your God-sized dream, make the most of where you are. Even when you're in the weeds, you can still find joy in your present situation. You don't have to wait until you reach your dream in order to find your joy. Sometimes we can fall into a when/then mindset. When I graduate from college, then I will be happy. When I get a better job, then I will be happy. When I find a spouse, then I will be happy. When I am out of debt, then I will be happy. When I have kids in the house, then I will be happy. When the kids are out of the house, then I will be happy. We get locked into a when/then way of living, and while we're waiting for the future destination, we miss out on our present joy.

It is good to have a God-sized dream. Where there's no hope for the future, there's no joy in the present. But you don't have to wait until you reach your dream in order to find your joy. You can learn to make the most of your present situation and find your joy even now.

It's important to find joy in the journey, because you need strength for the journey. In order for you to reach your destination you need strength, and if you hold onto your joy, you can hold onto your strength.

The Bible says, "The joy of the Lord is your strength" **(Nehemiah 8:10).**

With the help of God, you can enjoy the journey.
Sharpen the skills you have been given.
Be faithful with the opportunity you currently have.
Learn to enjoy the journey as well as the destination.

Bloom where you are planted.

 *reflection*

On the Job Training

1. Identify a few of your present responsibilities that seem insignificant. List them here.

2. The Apostle Paul writes, "Whatever you do, work at it with all your heart, as working for the Lord" (Colossians 3:23). Write out some action or attitude changes that might bring glory to God as you carry out these insignificant responsibilities.

3. Everyone has some "insignificant responsibilities." Think of a person in your life, (home, work, school, friends), whom you could encourage by acknowledging their effort. Who will you encourage and how will you do it?

4. Pray this prayer: *Lord, show me the importance of paying attention to details in even the smallest of jobs. I know that you see everything I do, when the boss is not looking, even when no one else sees. Help me to bloom where I am planted by giving my best in my present surroundings. Amen.*

chapter TEN ➡

chapter NINE
chapter TEN

Promise Keeper

"A promise made should be a promise kept."
— Steve Forbes
Editor-in-Chief of *Forbes Magazine*

chapter ELEVEN
chapter TWELVE

I heard about a dying man who gave each of his best friends -- a lawyer, doctor and clergyman -- an envelope containing $25,000 in cash to be placed in his coffin. One week later the man died and the friends each placed an envelope in the coffin. Several months later, the three friends came together again.

The clergyman confessed he only put $10,000 in the envelope and sent the rest to a mission's project. The doctor confessed his envelope had only $8,000 because he donated to a medical charity. The lawyer was outraged, "I am the only one who kept my promise to our dying friend. I want you both to know the envelope I placed in the coffin contained my own personal check for the entire $25,000."

When it comes to people and promises, it can be a very mixed bag. They may keep their promises or they may not keep their promises. But when it comes to God, He always keeps His promises. That is what we learn from the story of Joseph.

As we followed his journey, Joseph was promoted all the way to the top of the household. He was in charge of everything that went on outside of the house and everything that went on inside the house. If you look a little deeper into the reason he was promoted, it has to do with the promise of God. God had made a promise to Joseph's great-grandfather. The promise had to do with blessing.

God said to a man in the Bible by the name of Abraham, "I will bless you and I will make you a blessing and the families of the earth will be blessed through you" **(Genesis 12:2-3).**

And through his great-grandson, Joseph, it was starting to happen. In that household, Joseph was being blessed, and the household of another nation was being blessed though him.

When God makes a promise,
He always keeps that promise.
You can have confidence in the promises of God.

FAVOR OF GOD

The promise had to do with being blessed and being a blessing. That is the biggest reason Joseph was promoted to the top of the house. Joseph succeeded because he was blessed by God. If the favor of God is on you, it doesn't matter where you are. He can prosper you wherever you are. He can bless you right where you are.

If you belong to God, if you have surrendered your life to Him, if you have turned your life over to Him, you can find success right where you are. If God is with you and God is for you, it doesn't matter if you live in a place that doesn't know God and you work for a person who doesn't know God.

The most important question is not
where you are —
The most important question is
whose you are.

The Bible says, "The Lord was with Joseph and gave him success" **(Genesis 39:2-3).**

In His last words to the disciples,
Jesus says, "I am with you always" **(Matthew 28:20).**

Say these words out loud, "The Lord is with me."

⋑ *my dad's story* ⋐

Faith Temple, San Jose

My dad, Kenny Foreman, told me when he left the church he had started in Kansas City to become the pastor of the church in San Jose, he prayed, "God, please do not take Your blessing from me. I will go where You want me to go as long as your blessing is with me." There were those who told my dad he should stay at the church in Kansas City.

My dad had planted his church in Kansas City eight years before, and it was doing very well. When he was asked to come to San Jose, there were those who told my dad the Bay Area was a graveyard for churches, but my dad knew it is the blessing of God that makes the difference.

If the blessing of God is with you, then it doesn't matter where you are. It is not where you are that is most important. It is whose you are that is most important.

Dad moved to San Jose, and God gave him favor in San Jose. Because of the blessing of God, the church has expanded every decade for five decades now.

God can give you increase in the ⬚ you have.

(Choose one or more to fill in the bank)

INFLUENCE	RESPONSIBILITY	OPPORTUNITY
AUTHORITY	POWER	POSITION

Do the best with what you have and pray God will give you increase. If the blessing of God is with you, where you are is not the most important question—it is whose you are that is most important. He can promote you in the middle of a place that doesn't know God, working for a man who doesn't know God. If He blesses you, not only will you be blessed but others will take notice of the blessing.

You will be a blessing to others.

"The house was blessed because of Joseph" **(Genesis 39:5).**

That is one of the reasons God blesses you. He wants you to be blessed. But He wants more than that. He wants others to be blessed because of you.

When He blesses you, it is about you, but it is about more than you.

He blesses you so you can be a blessing. Your computer company is being blessed because God has put His blessing on you. Your real estate company is being blessed because God has put His blessing on you. Your class is being blessed because God has put His blessing on you. Your household is being blessed because God has put His blessing on you. Your neighborhood is being blessed because God has put His blessing on you.

GOD BLESSES YOU

BE A BLESSING TO OTHERS.

*His blessing is about you,
but it is more than that—
it is about those around you.*

It's a little bit like throwing a rock into the water at the lake. If you take a rock and throw it into the water, the first thing that happens is there's the splash. If it's a big rock, then it makes a big splash. Then there are the ripples. The rock will create ripples that reach far beyond the splash. The ripples can reach all the way across the lake. When God drops His favor into your life, first there is the splash, and then there are the ripples. The ripples reach far beyond the splash. He blesses you, and then His blessing reaches far beyond you.

The ripples of the blessing wash over those around you — all the way to the other side of the lake.

❧ *Oral Lee Brown* ❧

ORAL LEE BROWN

One lady made waves when she had a heart to be a blessing to the at-risk kids in her hometown of Oakland, California. Statistics showed three-fourths of the kids who attended school in that district wouldn't graduate from high school.

Oral Lee Brown is a person of faith and took a step of faith to do something about it. She promised one of the first grade classes in her city if they would graduate from high school with a "C" average, she would find a way to pay for them to attend college. At the time, she made around $45,000 a year, but she believed God wanted her to be a blessing and would help her to be a blessing. Out of that first grade class, 19 of the 23 in the class went on to graduate from school and God blessed Oral Lee in a way that she could send them to college. She continues to help kids today through the foundation she created.

The blessing is about you. But is more than about you. It is so the blessing can rub off on those around you.

On the way to your God-sized dream, be a blessing to those around you.

 *reflection*

Promise Keeper

1. Make a list of some of God's blessings in your life.

2. Knowing we are "blessed to be a blessing," what are some ways you could use the blessings of God in your life to be a blessing to others?

3. It's easy for us to think we "deserve" or "earn" the blessings we have been given. The reality is, "the Lord is with you." Look back over the list of blessings you wrote and specifically thank God for each of them.

4. Pray this prayer: *Lord, You are the giver of all good things. Give me a grateful heart so I may be a channel through whom Your blessings can flow to others. I don't want to be a hoarder of blessings. I acknowledge I would not have these blessings without You. Help me to cooperate with You so Your promises can come to pass in my life and those around me. Amen.*

chapter ELEVEN

chapter NINE
chapter TEN
chapter ELEVEN

Wind Chill

"I generally avoid temptation unless I can't resist it."

— Mae West, Movie Actress

chapter TWELVE

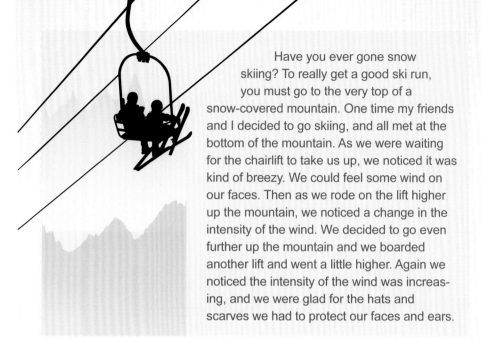

Have you ever gone snow skiing? To really get a good ski run, you must go to the very top of a snow-covered mountain. One time my friends and I decided to go skiing, and all met at the bottom of the mountain. As we were waiting for the chairlift to take us up, we noticed it was kind of breezy. We could feel some wind on our faces. Then as we rode on the lift higher up the mountain, we noticed a change in the intensity of the wind. We decided to go even further up the mountain and we boarded another lift and went a little higher. Again we noticed the intensity of the wind was increasing, and we were glad for the hats and scarves we had to protect our faces and ears.

The closer we got to the top of the mountain, the fiercer the wind came against us. When we reached the top of the mountain, the wind was blowing so hard, my teeth felt like they were coming loose.

The same thing can happen when you're on your way to your dream. The closer you get to the top, the harder the wind of temptation is going to blow around you.

Talk to a professional athlete, a corporate executive, and even a spiritual leader. Ask them about the temptations they face. They will tell you the wind really howls when you are at the top. Anyone who thinks he is beyond temptation, exempt from temptation, or can handle temptation on his own is setting himself up for a fall. All you have to do is check out the headlines in the paper.

Our confidence is not in our own strength but in the strength of God to help us overcome.

On the way to your God-sized dream, the higher you get, the harder the wind will howl.

temptation

Joseph was promoted all the way to the top position in the home of his master, and that is when temptation came looking for him. He was a handsome young man and the very attractive wife of his boss had her eye on him. She put the moves on him, didn't pull any punches, and told him exactly what her intentions were. She was what you might call a "cougar," and she had her sights set on her prey. She was out of her cage, out on the prowl, and her target was Joseph.

The Bible says, "His master's wife took notice of Joseph and said, 'Come to bed with me'" **(Genesis 39:7).**

No need to read between the lines. No need to wonder what she wants. She does not beat around the bush. She cuts right to the chase.

On the way to his dream, Joseph is hit in the face with the wind of temptation.

Everybody knows what it's like to be tempted. There is a T-shirt that reads, "I can resist everything except temptation." When you're on your way to your dream and you run into temptation, how will you resist it? How can you overcome it?

As we start to uncover the secrets of resisting and overcoming temptation, it might be helpful to get a handle on what temptation is. Temptation is defined as a cause or occasion of enticement.

Temptation is not desire.
The problem is not with desire.
God has given you certain desires.

"God wants to give you the desires of your heart" **(Psalm 37:4).**

There are God-given desires you have in your heart. There is the right way and the wrong way to fulfill each of those desires. When you break it down to its simplest form, temptation tries to lure you down the path of fulfilling a God-given desire the wrong way.

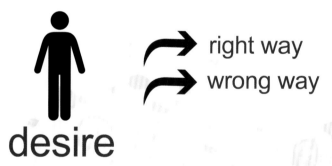

desire   right way / wrong way

Take for example the temptation of Joseph by his master's wife. There is nothing wrong with sexual desire. When God created human beings He created them with sexual desire. It's not the basic desire that's the problem. It's when you try to fulfill that desire in a distorted way.

The temptation of Joseph by his master's wife was an effort to lure him down that distorted, wrong path. This was a guy in his twenties, with all of that testosterone flowing through his body, and yet he is still able to run away from the temptation. Day after day she'd say to him, "Come to bed with me." But he refused and tried to stay as far away from her as he could. One day she became so aggressive she grabbed his coat and said,

"Come to bed with me."

The Bible says, "He tore himself away, but left his cloak in her hand as he ran from the house" **(Genesis 39:12 NLT).**

I've heard it said there's a time to stand and fight and there's a time to turn and run.

Joseph had the wisdom to turn and run when this temptation threatened to overpower him.

Poor Joseph. It seems he was always losing his coat. His brothers took his coat of many colors from him when they threw him in the pit. Then his boss' wife took another coat from him when he chose to run away from temptation. This poor guy kept losing his coat. But through it all he held onto his character. Others may take your coat from you, but they cannot take your character from you if you hold fast and stay strong. When you are on the way to your dreams, those winds will howl around you, but the Bible confirms,

"God is faithful; he will not let you be tempted beyond what you can bear. But when you are tempted, He will also provide a way out so that you can endure it" **(1 Corinthians 10:13 AMP).**

One of the men in our church said when he was just a kid he had the seed of a dream to be a lawyer planted in his heart. However, in the course of time he decided to take a different track and became an accountant. He did number crunching for a while, but that childhood dream was still stirring in his heart. He decided to go to law school. He worked very hard and finished at the top of his class, graduating from a prestigious law school. He landed a job with a top law firm. However, he found it was a difficult place for a Christian to work. He had partners who attempted to sabotage him in front of his clients, and he had clients fire him because he refused to lie. Other clients fired him saying they felt he was not tough enough because he refused to use profanity.

Through it all he refused to give in to the temptation. With the help of God, he stayed true to his faith, he stayed true to his values, and he stayed true to his convictions.

He writes,

"WHEN IT CAME TIME FOR THE FIRM TO PROMOTE PARTNERS FROM MY CLASS, I WAS THE ONLY ONE WHO MADE IT. NOT BY MY STRENGTHS BUT BY GOD'S."

God continued to bless him and give him favor in the workplace, and today he is the Deputy Athletic Director and Chief Legal Counsel for Stanford University's Athletic Department. He has also played a big part in helping us with our charter school project at our church.

On the way to your dream, the wind of temptation is going to hit you in the face. But with the help of God, it is possible to resist temptation and to overcome temptation.

See yourself standing firm.
See yourself standing strong.
See yourself standing your ground on top of the mountain!

Wind Chill

1. The Apostle Paul writes, "Be aware of the devil's schemes" (2 Corinthians 2:11, Ephesians 6:7). Paul is admonishing us to prepare for the ways that our enemy, the devil, might try to tempt us and take us off course. Write out some areas the devil has attacked you in the past, and is coming against you at present.

2. When you board a plane, the flight attendant goes over the "exit strategy" in case of emergency. What is your "exit strategy" when temptation comes?

3. List a few friends who could help you be accountable with your "exit strategy."

4. Say this prayer: *Lord, I thank You that You will not allow me to be tempted beyond what I am able to bear. Help me to cooperate with You when the winds of temptation start to blow. I know everyone has blind spots and I ask You to protect me and bring people around me who will help me be strong. Amen.*

chapter TWELVE

- chapter NINE
- chapter TEN
- chapter ELEVEN
- chapter TWELVE

Off The Hook

"You cannot keep birds from flying over your head, but you can keep them from building a nest in your hair."

— **Martin Luther,** Theologian and Reformer

On the way to his dream, Joseph resisted temptation and overcame temptation. Here are a few things to help you when you encounter temptation. They all start with the word *focus*. What you *focus* on is important. It is a little bit like this picture.

The cat is focused on the fish. If the cat continues to focus on the fish, the fish will not be in the bowl for long. The cat will have sushi for dinner.

The more you focus on a temptation, the harder it is to resist the temptation, the stronger you will feel the pull of it. You may not be able to keep temptation from focusing in on you, but you do not have to focus in on the temptation. You can shift your focus somewhere else. By shifting your focus somewhere else, you will break the power of the temptation.

What you focus on is important.
focus
focus
focus

When I am trying to drop a few pounds, I have to stay away from chocolate cake. If there is a chocolate cake in the house and I start looking at that chocolate cake, it is just a matter of time until that chocolate cake puts a fork in my hand and a bite in my mouth. Then, I am on my way to the store to buy some bigger pants.

What you **focus** on is important. The more you **focus** on a temptation, the harder it is to resist the temptation, and the stronger you will feel its pull. The stronger you will feel the draw of it. You may not be able to keep the temptation from focusing on you, but you do not have to **focus** on the temptation. You can shift your **focus** somewhere else.

By shifting your focus somewhere else, it will help to break the power of the temptation.

When temptation comes, if you allow yourself to **focus** on the temptation, you are on your way to giving in. Do you remember way back in the Garden of Eden how Eve was tempted to eat the forbidden fruit? When she looked at and **focused** on the forbidden fruit, nothing else seemed to matter; nothing else seemed to exist. As soon as it grabbed her **focus**, she was on her way to taking a bite.

If you **focus** on the temptation with your eyes or with your thoughts, it is just a matter of time until you are on your way to taking a bite. The more you **focus** on the temptation, the more you are drawn to it. Your life tends to lean toward the direction of your **focus**.

Shift the focus away from the temptation and your life will lean away from it. It will help you to break the power of temptation.

When temptation shows up on your way to your dream, instead of focusing on the temptation, direct your focus toward God. The more you **focus** on the temptation, God will seem less present to you. God will seem very distant to you. God will even seem less real to you. When you shift your focus toward God, you remind yourself He is with you, and He is for you, and He can give you power to resist the temptation. That is what Joseph did.

We know this because he said to the wife, "How could I do such a wicked thing and sin against God?" **(Genesis 39:9).**

Joseph redirected his thoughts from the cougar who is in front of him, to the lion who is above him - the God who had delivered him and given him favor in his master's house.

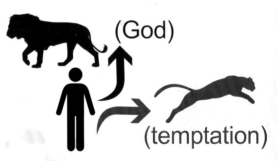

Here is the formula for resisting and overcoming temptation:

- Think about how good God has been to you.
- Think about how much God has done for you.
- Find a scripture that tells you how much you matter to God.
- Remind yourself God loves you so much He sent His only Son to die for you.

If you keep your focus on God, no matter what is tempting you, you will resist the temptation.

When temptation shows up on your way to your God-sized dream, instead of focusing on the temptation, redirect your **focus** toward the truth. When temptation shows up, it will never tell you the truth. Temptation always looks good, but it is not the truth. It is a little bit like fishing. When you are fishing, you take your pole and put a hook at the end of the line. Next, you take some bait and you do your best to hide the hook. Then, you put the line in the water and the fish swim by and see the bait. The bait looks good, and the bait smells good. When the fish takes the bait, it finds out there is a hook inside the bait. The same thing is true when it comes to temptation.

There is a hook inside that bait.

Temptation will not tell you about the hook. It will not let you see the hook. It will try and hide the hook. But when you take the bait, there is always a hook inside. One of the best things you can do to resist temptation is to shift your focus from the lie to the truth.

Remind yourself there is a hook inside that bait.

You may even want to take out a piece of paper, and write down the truth about the bait. What is the hook inside the bait? If you give in to this temptation, write out the trouble this will cause your family, or your career, or your health, or your reputation, or your self-esteem, or your finances, or your conscience, or your future. There is a hook inside the bait. What is the hook inside the bait? It will cause you pain; it will cause those around you pain. Shift your focus from the lie to the truth.

Jesus once said, "You will know the truth and the truth will set you free" **(John 8:32).**

When temptation shows up on your way to your dream, redirect your focus toward the dream, instead of focusing on the temptation.

There is a popular band called "Family Force 5." They play a style of music referred to as "crunk rock." It is a diverse blend of styles such as punk, rap, funk, and electronica. Their music is featured on dance charts, movie sound tracks, video game releases, and has won several different awards. The band was once asked about how they deal with all the temptations that come with the music industry. They revealed what has helped them is their dream.

They have a dream God will use their music to influence young people in a positive way. They believe God has a plan and purpose for their music, and as long as they stay focused on that dream it helps them to stay out of trouble.

When you keep your eyes on the dream in front of you, it will help you resist temptation. If there is a God-sized dream in your heart of what you can be and what you can do, that dream is much too important to throw away on temptation. The dream is too important to God, too important to you, and too important to others to throw away on temptation. You know where you are headed. You refuse to take your eyes off your dream. You can be so focused on your dream that even when temptation hones in on you, it doesn't have the power to change your focus.

Saying a loud "Yes!" to your dream from God helps to say a loud "No!" to temptation.

There is power in a God-sized dream to break the power of temptation.

❧ Tim Brown ❧

TIM BROWN

NFL Hall of Fame finalist Tim Brown visited our church, and shared a bit about fame and success with our congregation. As a professional football player, the wind blows very hard on top of that mountain. Every time you turn around, you are hit with it.

Tim is a great example of how, when God gives you success, you can stay centered. Tim believes God let him achieve success on the football field to be an example to other players. "God didn't have me playing at a high level because He wanted me to be in the Hall of Fame," he said. "He wanted me to show these young guys that you can play at a very high level but you can still serve God."

For example, being such a high profile, world-class athlete, there are plenty of opportunities for men to be unfaithful to their wives, having affairs with other women. That short-lived pleasure can have long-term consequences. There is always a hook inside that bait. The temptation is a powerful one, but keeping your focus on God can give you the strength to resist the temptation and be faithful to your wife.

He told our congregation, "When I met my wife, she had a lot of hang ups about athletes, because all she had heard was you could have this great life, but you're going to have to deal with extra women being in the relationship," Tim said. "The thing I told her was, you don't have to worry about me doing that kind of stuff, because I will always love God more than I will love you."

With his family and his faith, he was able to keep his perspective, stay grounded and overcome temptation — even on top of the mountain.

SCAN: The interview with Tim Brown is available through this QR code, or go to www.cathedraloffaith.org/timbrown

reflection

Off The Hook

1. What is the bait that tends to grab your attention?

2. Write out the truth about the bait that lures you, and identify the trouble that would come about should you take a bite.

3. Ask God to give you a truth from Scripture to help you overcome the lies and temptations you might encounter. Write it out here. (Here are some sample verses: Joshua 1:9, Psalm 32:8, 55:22, 84:11, Romans 15:13, 1 Corinthians 2:9, Philippians 1: 6, Hebrews 13:20,21, and James 1:5).

4. Pray this prayer: *Lord, open my eyes to see through the lies that would tempt me away from fulfilling Your dream for my life. Keep me focused on You, on Your words, on Your dream. I don't want to settle for less than Your best. I know You will complete this work You have started in me. I look to You for my strength. Amen.*

section IV ➡

Section 4:
Prison Break

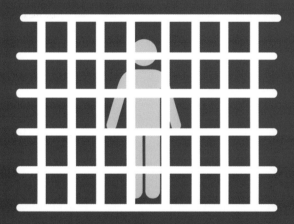

"He took Joseph and threw him into prison where the king's prisoners were held, and there he remained" (Genesis 39:20 NLT).

chapter THIRTEEN

Writing
On The Wall

"There is no pit so deep that God's love is
not deeper still."
— Corrie Ten Boom, Holocaust Survivor

chapter FOURTEEN
chapter FIFTEEN
chapter SIXTEEN

I'm a big Oakland Raiders fan, and there's a place at the Raider's stadium known as the 'Black Hole.' It can be a pretty rough and tough area, but I'm always up for a football game and someone gave me tickets — located in the Black Hole. As my friend and I made our way to our seats, we noticed someone sitting in them. We mentioned it to an usher, and the guy in our seats stood up and seemed a little intense. He looked at the usher and screamed something like, "You better make sure that you get this right, because I don't mind going back to prison!" Welcome to the Black Hole. It's one thing to be in prison because you deserve it. It is another thing to be there when you don't. Life doesn't always seem fair.

My friend James Romero & me

One of my favorite movies is *The Count of Monte Cristo.* In the movie, the lead character is accused of a crime he didn't commit and is thrown into prison. When in prison, his faith is tested. He doesn't deserve to be there. It's not fair he's in that prison. At first, he believes God is with him even in the prison. In the prison, someone has written on the wall, "God will give me justice." But the longer he is in prison the more he starts to wonder if the writing on the wall is correct. Has God forgotten him? Has God forsaken him? What if he is alone in the prison? What if the writing on the wall really says God is nowhere in the prison?

As he wrestles with his faith, he has a conversation with another prisoner—a priest who is also wrongly imprisoned. During the conversation, the priest mentions God. The lead character says he does not believe in God. The priest replies,

"It doesn't matter. He believes in you."

On the way to your God-sized dream, you will encounter situations when life doesn't seem fair. That's the kind of moment the young man Joseph faced. As we've followed his story, we've seen he had a dream that one day he would be a leader. On the way to his dream, though, life didn't treat him fairly. The wife of his boss tried to seduce him, but he refused to sleep with her. So, she lied about him and accused him of trying to force himself on her.

The Bible says she told her husband, "That Hebrew slave you've brought into our house tried to come in and fool around with me" **(Genesis 39:17 NLT).** (And you thought the Bible was boring.)

Joseph went to prison for a crime he didn't commit. He did the right thing and ended up in prison. It's one thing to go prison for doing the wrong thing. He went to prison for doing the right thing. I wonder what he was thinking and how he was feeling while sitting in a prison cell knowing he did the right thing. What do you think he was asking?

HAS EVERYONE FORSAKEN ME?

HAVE I BEEN FORGOTTEN?

AM I ALL ALONE?

WHERE IS GOD IN ALL OF THIS?

IS PRISON THE FINALE OF MY LIFE? AM I STUCK HERE FOREVER?

The writing on the prison wall seemed to read, "God is nowhere."

And yet it's interesting. If you take those same letters in the word *nowhere* and make a small change, there is a major shift in the meaning and the message.

"nowhere" becomes "now here."

That is the message in the story of Joseph. The writing was on the wall of his life. Life wasn't fair to him. But God had not forsaken him. God had not abandoned him. The prison cell could keep Joseph in, but it couldn't keep God out.

The Bible says, "The Lord was with Joseph in the prison and showed him His faithful love" **(Genesis 39:21 NLT).**

The writing is on the wall of your life as well, even when life isn't fair and you're in the darkest prison. Yeah, the facts may be you are in a prison,

but the truth is:

- **God has not abandoned you.**
- **God has not forsaken you.**
- **You are not alone in the dark, in the storm, in the crisis.**
- **God is still with you and always for you.**
- **God is now here.**

As you are reading this chapter, maybe you feel orphaned, abandoned, friend-less, family-less, spouse-less, job-less, health-less, or companion-less. You feel like you're in the dark. On the way to your dream, you find yourself without even a candle to curse the darkness. Your situation…

I was talking with a couple recently and that's how they were feeling. They were in the dark. They are married and have a dream to have a child. They've been trying for eight years, but they had not been able to have a child. It reached a point where they're frustrated and confused. They watched their friends have children. Yet they were not able to have children of their own. The doctors didn't have an answer. Why?

Life simply wasn't fair.

They loved God and did their best to trust and serve Him. That's what made the situation confusing to them. If a person doesn't believe in God, there's no reason to be confused. Without God, there's no such thing as what is right or what it is fair. But because we believe in God, when life doesn't seem fair, that's when it can get confusing.

You may feel right now like you're in the dark. In fact, as you finish this chapter, turn out the lights and read it in the dark. You may need a flashlight or your cell phone to help you. At one point or another, everyone faces unfair circumstances. Life doesn't seem just, and we sit in a cell imprisoned by unfulfilled expectations, hopes, and dreams.

Here's what I've discovered. When you feel like you're in the dark, you can lock in on what you don't know and become more confused. Or, you can lock in on what you do know and that will lead to clarity. You still may not have all the answers but you do have the **Answer**.

GOD ALONE IS THE ANSWER.

God says, "I will never leave you, I will never forsake you" (**Hebrews 13:5**).

EVEN WHEN YOU'RE IN THE DARK

It's a little bit like running into a fog bank.

We were once on a boat crossing the San Francisco Bay and ran into a fog bank. It was the kind of fog bank in which you could barely see your hand in front of your face. If you're on the water and encounter such a dense fog, it's easy to get confused. You're not sure where you are or where you're headed, if you aren't careful, you can run into the rocks and end up with a shipwreck on your hands. But if the fog was to lift, or if you were lifted above the fog, you would quickly find clarity.

On the way to your dream,
when you run into the fog bank,
lock in on what you do know.

If you lock in on what you don't know, you may shipwreck your faith. Lock in on what you do know, rise up in faith above the fog. You may not know everything, but you know the God who knows all things.

Most importantly,
He has a good plan and future for you.
You know you are in Christ and with Him,
you're never alone in the dark.
God will never leave you or forsake you.

When you feel like you're in the dark, don't follow your feelings, which feel real but they are not reality. Instead, follow your faith. In the dark, your feelings can be all over the map. One moment you can feel this way. The next moment you can feel that way. Don't follow your feelings.

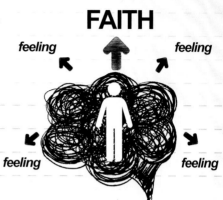

Don't deny what you feel;
just refuse to follow what you feel.

Feelings make good servants, but they are bad masters. Instead of following your feelings, you follow your faith.

C.S. Lewis once described faith this way, "Faith is the art of holding onto things that your reason has once accepted in spite of your changing moods."

When you're in the dark, your moods may change this way and that way. But don't follow your feelings — follow your faith. With eyes of faith, you know He is with you and for you. He will never leave you, abandon you, forget you, ignore you, or forsake you. The one thing you can know in the dark is you are not alone.

I heard about a little boy whose mom asked him to get the broom out of the closet. The boy said he didn't want to get the broom out of the closet. The closet was dark; he didn't like the dark and was afraid of the dark. His mom told him God would be with him—God was even there in the dark. The little boy walked over to the closet. He opened the door and looked into the dark. Then he said,

"GOD, IF YOU ARE THERE IN THE CLOSET, WOULD YOU PLEASE HAND ME THE BROOM?"

The dark can be a scary place if you're all alone. But if you're not alone, the dark isn't so scary anymore. When you feel you're in the dark, look with eyes of faith and know He's with you. The dark is still dark, but it's not as scary anymore.

The Bible says in the dark "God is there ready to help" **(Psalm 46:1 GNT).**

**On the way to your dream,
when you run into the dark,
the writing is on the wall.
The writing is this —**

God is now here.

Writing on the Wall

1. Turn to Psalm 139 and read it out loud. Close your Bible, and write out here the key thoughts and phrases from this passage that the Holy Spirit highlights to you.

2. Write down any ways you feel like you're in the dark, whether it is a situation you are facing, or a dream you are pursuing. Then, find a room where you can turn out the lights and sit in the dark. Take a few moments to sit quietly in the dark. Because God is "now here" with you, ask Him if there is anything He wants to say to you "in the dark."

3. Pray this prayer out loud: *Lord, I thank You that Your Word is a light to shine into my darkness. I ask You to illuminate me with the knowledge that You are with me. You will never leave me or forsake me. Help me to see my life and circumstances from Your perspective as You continue to release and fulfill Your dream in my life. Amen.*

chapter FOURTEEN ➡️

chapter THIRTEEN
chapter FOURTEEN

The aXe
Factor

"The way anything is developed is through practice, practice, practice, practice, practice, practice, practice, practice, practice and more practice."

— Joyce Meyer, Author & Speaker

chapter FIFTEEN
chapter SIXTEEN

The America's Cup was in the San Francisco Bay area recently. It is the number one sailing competition in the world. Watching the boats cut through the water and around the course was exciting. The boats would head one way, turn around the buoy and then head back the other way toward another buoy. They would continue to do this until they crossed the finished line.

One thing really fascinates me about sailing—using the wind. I don't know much about sailing. I've only been on a sailboat a couple of times. One time the captain let me take the helm, and I almost ran

us into the rocks. But I enjoy sailing and watching those who sail. One thing that's fascinating to me is it doesn't seem to matter which way the wind is blowing. You can use wind to sail one way and you can turn the boat around and use the same wind to sail another way.

It's not the wind's direction that matters most; how you set the sail determines the direction of the boat.

The same thing is true in life. You can put two people in the same wind. You can put them in the same environment. You can put them in the same circumstance. One of them will go this way and one of them will go that way.

Two people can live in the same home, have the same parents, receive the same upbringing, one of them goes this way and one of them goes that way. Two people can go to the same college, have the same teachers, take the same classes, one of them goes this way and one of them goes that way. Two people can go to the same job, have the same manager, with the same responsibility. One of them goes this way and one of them goes that way. Even when it comes to adversity, two people can face the same difficulty—the same challenge—and one of them goes this way, one of them goes that way. It's not the wind that matters most; it's how you set the sail that determines the direction of the boat.

This was true in the life of Joseph.

On the way to his dream, it didn't matter which way the wind was blowing. Time and again he faced the wind of adversity. He was thrown into a pit and then he was hit with temptation. After that, he was falsely accused and thrown into prison. Yet each time he was hit with adversity, he was the one who set the sail and determined which way the wind would take him. While he was in prison, he made the best of a bad situation and rose to the top.

The Bible says, "The warden put Joseph in charge of all the other prisoners and over everything that happened in the prison. The warden had no more worries, because Joseph took care of everything. The Lord was with him and caused everything he did to succeed" **(Genesis 39:22-23 NLT).**

It happened again and again. The wind blew, Joseph (not others or the situation) set the sail, and it moved Joseph closer to his dream. Fatalists, negative thinkers, skeptics and doubters are driven off course by the wind; believers, positive thinkers, and dreamers harness the wind and stay on course, on purpose with God!

Joseph had a dream to be a leader and in the prison he had a chance to develop the gift he had been given.

When you are born, you are given certain gifts. Those gifts are connected to the dream God has for your life. He gives you those gifts so you can fulfill the dream.

139

One former boxing champion, **Sugar Ray Leonard,** was speaking to a group of college students. He said to them, "I consider myself blessed — I consider you blessed — we have all been blessed with God-given talents. Mine just happens to be beating people up."

When you're born, you have been given a talent. The talent you have is connected to your dream. God gives you the talent you need so you can achieve the dream He has for your life. On the way to your dream, it's important to discover the talent you've been given. Ask God to help you to see. Ask others to help you to see. Trial and error can also help you to see.

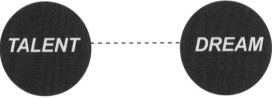

TALENT - - - - - - - - - - DREAM

 Discovering the talent you have is the first step.

 Developing the talent you have is the second step.

In one place, the Bible gives an interesting picture of this. It says, "If the axe and its edge are unsharpened, more strength is needed, but skill will bring success" **(Ecclesiastes 10:10).** A dull axe is not very effective. A dull axe is not very productive, but a sharp axe will give you the edge.

The same thing is true when it comes to your talent. God has given you the talent to fulfill the dream He has for your life, and yet, the talent has to be grown. The talent has to be developed. The talent has to be sharpened.

Sharpen the talent you have and it will give you the edge. It will give you the winning edge.

In prison, Joseph continued to develop the leadership gift he had been given. One day it would give him the winning edge.

What can you do to sharpen the axe you have been given?

Find a friend, mentor or coach who can help you to sharpen the axe. I was talking to a vocal coach recently who helps some of the top singers in the world prepare for their concerts. It struck me that these top singers have a vocal coach. Even people at the top of their game have a coach.

If you want to make the most of your talent, find a coach. Find a person from whom you can learn. Find people who can help you grow. They may do what you want to do. They may be good at what you want to be good at doing. They may know how to help you excel at what you do. Watch what they do. Read about what they do. Talk to them. Learn from them. Listen to them. Find a good coach who will help you to sharpen the axe.

When you sharpen the axe, it can give you the winning edge.

You can grow from a failure or a mistake.

One teen boy came home from a football game. It was late and he was surprised to see his dad was still up. He saw his father had crashed the computer and was fumbling around trying to figure out what to do. This is what the teenager said, "Dad, you are quite natural at multi-tasking; you can stay up and goof up all at the same time."

If you're like me and you struggle with perfectionism, then you probably hate to goof up as much as I do. And yet, what I have come to realize is goofing up is one of the ways you can sharpen the axe. Failure is not fun, but if you learn from the failure and grow from the failure, when it is all said and done, you're a little bit smarter—a little bit wiser—and your axe is a little bit sharper because of the failure.

When you sharpen the axe,
it will give you the winning edge.

Practice can help you to sharpen the axe.

According to the book *Outliers*, for a person to become an expert at something, it not only takes talent, it takes 10,000 hours of practice. This seems to hold true no matter what the field, whether it's in computers or sports or music or science. It's good to have talent, but talent alone will not make you an expert. It takes a whole lot of practice, and it seems 10,000 hours is when you hit the threshold. You may have more than 10,000 hours under your belt. You may have less than 10,000 hours under your belt.

The point is, get as much practice as you can under your belt. It will help you to sharpen the axe.

The Bible says, "Do you see someone skilled in his or her work? They will serve before kings" **(Proverbs 22:29)**.

A sharp axe can give you the winning edge when it comes to your dream.

The aXe Factor

1. God has given you talents and gifts. Write down the ones you have already discovered.

2. For each talent you have discovered, write out several ways you can develop those gifts.

3. Pray this prayer: *Lord, You are the giver of all good gifts. You have blessed me with relationships, experiences, and skills which You want me to use for Your glory. I commit myself to serving You. Show me the plan You have for me. Give me Your perspective on my 'windy' days so that I may sail into Your purpose for my life. Amen.*

chapter FIFTEEN ➡

chapter THIRTEEN
chapter FOURTEEN
chapter FIFTEEN

Dream Releaser

> "Really great people make you feel that you, too, can become great."
> — **Mark Twain**, Author and Humorist

chapter SIXTEEN

I heard a story about a couple recently married. The husband came home one night to find his wife crying. With tears coming down her cheeks, she said, "The dog ate the dinner, the dog ate the dinner." The husband put his arm around his wife and said, "Honey, don't worry about it— we'll just get another dog."

On the way to his dream, Joseph is thrown into prison. While he's in prison there are two other men thrown into prison. Both of these men worked for the king and were involved in the food service. We aren't sure exactly what happened, but it seems something went wrong with one of the meals and they were thrown into prison because of it. One night while in prison, both of them had dreams. Joseph interpreted the dreams for them.

Joseph said to them, "Tell me your dreams" **(Genesis 40:8).**

With the help of God, he interpreted their dreams, which eventually led to his release from prison.

If you're only interested in reaching your own dream, then your thinking is too small. Think about how you can help others with their dreams.

How can you use your influence to help them with their dreams?

How can you use what you have been given to help them with their dreams?

How can you inspire others to help them with their dreams?

How can you build up others to help them with their dreams?

When you get excited about making someone else successful, this is one of the best things you can do on the way to your dream. Don't get so wrapped up with your dream you forget to help others with their dream.

One of the great joys you will have in life is when you become a dream releaser.

When you help others with their dream, you are on the way to reaching your dream.

Joel Osteen writes, "What you make happen for others God will make happen for you."

There's a picture I've seen which caught my attention. The picture is of a turtle on a fence post. There's a caption under the picture that reads,

"If you see a turtle on a fence post, you know he had some help."

All of us need a little help if we're going to climb higher. When I look back on my life, there are so many people who've helped me climb a little higher. There were those who spoke words of faith into my life. They would write me a note, send me a scripture or say a prayer. They would open a door, give me a chance, share some advice, or give me constructive feedback. They helped to bring out the best in me.

They believed in me and God used them to help me believe.

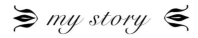
I think about one leader who's been a dream releaser for me, Bruce Wilkinson. This leader has written best-selling books and launched major ministries. He took me under his wing and helped me to dream. He helped me have faith to reach for those dreams and develop strategies to reach for those dreams. He's become a mentor and a friend to me and he's helped this turtle with that fence post. He has more than enough to do. He has his own dreams God has dropped in his heart. But that's the kind of man he is—he thinks about more than his own dreams. He takes an interest in the dreams of others. He took an interest in the dream God put in my heart. One of his favorite things to say is, "Is there something I can do for you?"

What if we looked at the people who are in our lives and asked that question—

What can I do for you?

It may mean helping to stir up the dream on the inside of them.

Jesus was always helping people to dream. He helped them to see more than what they were. He helped them see what they could be and what they could do. When Jesus met a certain man named Simon, Jesus changed his name to Peter. In those days names had meanings. The name Simon meant, "a reed that was blown back and forth by the wind." That was a pretty good description of who Simon was at that time. He was the kind of person who could be blown back and forth by the wind. He could be way over here one minute and way over there the next. He was not very reliable and not very dependable.

Jesus saw who he was, but He also saw who Simon could become. The name Peter means *rock*. A *rock* is reliable and dependable. Jesus changed Simon's name to help him see who he could become.

Simon

A Reed that was blown back and forth by the wind.

Peter

A Rock that is reliable and dependable.

When you look at others, see more than who they are. See who they can become with the help of God. Don't wait to believe in them after they're a success. Anyone can believe in them after they're a success. Believe in them before they are a success. Speak words that inspire and encourage them to dream. That's one of the ways you can help others with their dreams.

Let them know God has a dream for their life. With His help, they can reach their potential and fulfill their dream. The words you speak have power. The words you speak may be the thing that helps them to believe they can, in fact, have a dream and with the help of God, reach their dream. We all need some help to climb higher.

Who are the people God has put in your life that you could help with their dream?

I had the chance to visit the set of a major motion picture being produced about the life of Noah. The director of the movie told us about his vision for the movie and then a little bit of his personal story. When he was in middle school, he wrote a poem about Noah for one of his classes. He said the teacher in the class believed in him and his creativity, and had a major influence in his life. Her words of encouragement inspired him to believe he could be creative and follow the dream in his heart. He's gone on to become an award-winning director and is making this movie that's been in the works for a very long time.

His teacher is still alive and as a tribute to her for helping to release the dream in his life, he has given her a part in the movie. She probably never dreamed she would be in a movie, but she spoke words of faith that inspired someone to reach for their dream and now she is in a movie.

Who are the people God has put in your life that you could help with their dream?

Instead of thinking, "I wonder what these people can do for me?" think about what you can do for them. If you've been blessed with…

• A strong marriage → look for a hurting marriage and do what you can to help the couple restore it.
• The opportunity to go to college → look for a student and do what you can to help them get into college.
• Breaking an addiction → look for a person struggling with addiction and do what you can to help them break their addiction.
• Financial freedom → look for a person struggling financially and do what you can to help them to find financial freedom.
• Success in your career → look for a person struggling profession-ally and do what you can to help them have success in their career.
• A gift for creating music → look for a person interested in creating music and do what you can to help them create music.
• Faith to follow your dream → share your faith with others.

There is a person at my church who was once heavily into gangs. That was the path he was on. Then one day, he turned his life over to God and started down a different path. That's the kind of thing God does. If you're on one path, God can help you to start down a different path. Tony Ortiz started down a different path, and he started to help others head down a different path. He started to help others begin to dream there was a better life they could have. He has helped others get out of gangs. He has helped others avoid getting into gangs. He has helped them to dream about a different path and to follow a different path. Over the years, Tony has become well known for his expertise, and is sought out across the country by police chiefs and mayors. He has been given local, state, and national awards for the amazing work that he does. He has even been invited to the White House to discuss gang prevention in America.

When you help others with their dream, you are on your way to achieving your dream.

LIZ & TONY ORTIZ

 *reflection*

Dream Releaser

1. Write out the names of people God has put in your life you could help with their dream.

2. Write out some specific steps you could take to help them fulfill their God-sized dream.

3. Here's a prayer to pray: *God-sized dreams start with You, God. You give them and You help them come to pass. You send the right people at just the right time to say just the right thing. Let me be that right person for someone by serving them, encouraging them or providing for them. Help me be on the lookout for ways to release God-sized dreams in others. Amen.*

 **chapter SIXTEEN**

- chapter THIRTEEN
- chapter FOURTEEN
- chapter FIFTEEN
- **chapter SIXTEEN**

Waiting Game

"Somehow you'll escape all that waiting and staying. You'll find the bright places where Boom Bands are playing."

— **Dr. Seuss**, Writer and Artist

Oh, The Places You'll Go!

I heard about a family who was taking a long trip. After some time had passed, the little boy in the back seat asked, "Are we there yet?" The dad said, "No, we're not there yet." Some more time passed and the little boy asked, "Are we there yet?" The dad said, "No, we're not there yet." Some more time passed and the little boy said, "Dad, am I still going to be seven when we get there?"

On the way to your God-sized dream, it takes patience, persistence, and perseverance to reach your dream.

This is what we learn from the story of Joseph. It took patience and persistence for him to reach his dream. On the way to his dream he ran into one delay after another. It happened to him again while he was in prison. The person he helped out in prison promised Joseph when he got out of prison he would help Joseph. Eventually, he kept his promise and helped Joseph. But it didn't happen right away.

When the man got out of prison and got his old job back, he forgot all about Joseph for two years. Joseph had to wait two more years for help. He was stuck in that prison for two more years. It probably felt like twenty years. It had been many years since that dream of being a leader had first been dropped in his heart. He had been waiting a long time. Now he ran into yet another delay. It's not easy to run into delays. **It takes patience, perseverance, and persistence to reach the dream.**

| Patience | Perseverance | Persistence |

This is one of the hardest lessons for us to learn, because we live in a culture that hates to wait. No one really likes to wait. Whether it is in the airport, at the doctor's office, in the grocery store checkout line, at a restaurant, on the freeway or on the Internet, we hate to wait.

In one research study, they discovered the average person will :

wait 17 minutes in a store before they get impatient.

wait 9 minutes on the phone before they get impatient.

wait 20 minutes for a sermon to finish before they get impatient.

The last stat I made up myself, but it seems to be about right. It's not easy to be patient. I don't like to wait. You don't like to wait. That's why we have fast food and instant coffee, 24 hour dry cleaning, and overnight shipping.

We have a need for speed. We hate to wait.

The hardest place to wait is when you are on your way to your dream and you run into delays.
But when we run into delays, it's important to remember

delays are not denials.

It may take some time, more time than we wish it would take, but with patience and perseverance we will take hold of our God-sized dream. The bigger the dream and the bolder the dream, the more time it may take. But when you run into a delay, remember, delays are not denials.

The Bible says, "Imitate those who through faith and patience received what was promised" **(Hebrews 6:12).**

Faith gets us going toward our dream; patience keeps us moving toward our dream.

When you have a God-sized dream in your heart, it takes patience and perseverance to possess the promise. View your journey toward your dream as a marathon instead of a sprint. If you take on the mindset of a sprinter you will expect to reach the finish line quickly and if you don't, you will run out of breath and possibly give up the race. Take on the mindset of a marathon runner. It's not a sprint you're running; it's a marathon.

On the way to your dream, there are twists and turns. On the way to your dream, there are hills and valleys. On the way to your dream, there is a lot of territory to cover.

You know the finish line is out there. You know it will take some time to get there, but if you just keep putting one foot in front of the other you will cross the finish line. Who knows, it could be around the next turn. There may only be one more lap to go. If you are patient, persistent and you persevere, you will cross the finish line.

Take on the mindset of a marathon runner.

Here in the Silicon Valley, we are known for overnight successes. But, if you look closely at the way the companies in the Valley have taken off, most of the time what appears to be an overnight success didn't happen overnight. It may look like it happened overnight, but there have been many nights of patience, persistence, and perseverance behind that "overnight" success.

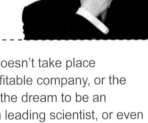

Marketing guru **Seth Godin** says, "It takes about six years of hard work to become an overnight success."

Most of the time an overnight success doesn't take place overnight. If it's the dream to build a profitable company, or the dream to make a blockbuster movie, or the dream to be an outstanding singer, or the dream to be a leading scientist, or even the dream to be a professional baseball player it may look like a person is an overnight success. But behind the overnight success there are usually many nights of blood, sweat, and tears.

It takes patience and perseverance to be an overnight success.

Recently, I received a note from a young lady. She and her husband were $30,000 in debt and tired of being slaves to it. If you're in a great deal of debt, it can feel like you're in bondage. That's what it felt like to them. They were tired of feeling trapped and they made a decision to get out of debt. It was a dream they had in their heart. They took a class we offer at the church. They put what they learned into practice and prayed God would help them get out of debt. Even though the economy was not in good shape, they were able to chip away at the debt. Five years later, they are an overnight success. They were aiming to be out of debt by the spring of 2013 but they received an unexpected check and were out of debt in the fall of 2012.

Stephanie wrote,

"GOD LIKES TO DO THINGS IN A WAY THAT LETS YOU KNOW HE IS GOD."

With the help of God, you can be an overnight success. It just may take you a few nights to get there.

One of the most persistent men in history has a record that reads this way:

At 21, he saw his first business fail.
At 23, he ran for a state political office and lost.
At 24, he saw his second business fail.
At 27, he had a nervous breakdown.
At 29, he ran for Congress and lost.
At 31, he ran for Congress and lost again.
At 37, he ran for Congress and won.
At 46, he ran for Vice President and lost.
At 49, he ran for the Senate and lost. After all of this, you would think he would walk off the track.

But he continued to show patience and persistence and perseverance, and **at the age of 51, Abraham Lincoln became the sixteenth President of the United States.**

One of the keys to patience and perseverance is to keep your eye on the prize. Don't lose sight of your dream.

my story

MY DAUGHTER LAUREN (ON THE LEFT)

Many years ago when I was teaching my daughter how to swim, she would get in the water and I would stand a few feet in front of her. She would start swimming toward me and I would say, "You can do it, Lauren." She would take a few strokes and then she would look up at me and I would say, "Come on, Lauren, you can do it," and she did. She kept swimming and she kept seeing. She kept swimming and she kept seeing, until she made it all the way to the other side of the pool. As long as she kept seeing, she kept swimming.

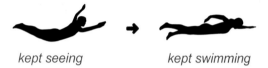

kept seeing → *kept swimming*

The same thing is true when it comes to our dreams. As long as we keep seeing, we will keep moving forward.

Perhaps you need to "see" this promise from God written by the Apostle Paul,

"I can do all things through Christ who strengthens me" **(Philippians 4:13).**

At the church we often speak that promise as a ten-finger prayer. Hold up your hands and say each of the words of this promise as you flex a finger.

Do the exercise again as you say this promise out loud.

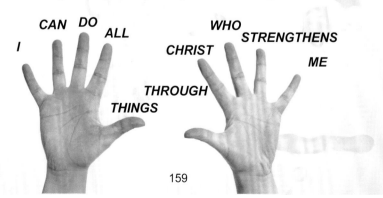

I CAN DO ALL THINGS THROUGH CHRIST WHO STRENGTHENS ME

If all we see are the delays, it is easy to get down, depressed and discouraged. But, if we keep our eyes on our dream and the God who gave us the dream, we can keep moving forward.

Jesus was able to put up with anything because of His vision. He had a vision to save the world and because of His vision, He could even put up with death on the cross.

The Bible says Jesus endured the suffering of the cross "because of the joy that was awaiting Him" **(Hebrews 12:2 NLT).**

Keep the dream you have in front of you. See yourself reaching the dream; see yourself achieving the dream.

When you keep the dream in front of you, you can deal with difficulties; you can handle the delays. As long as you keep seeing, you can keep swimming, all the way to the end of the pool.

With patience, persistence, and perseverance you can reach your dream!

Kenny Foreman

Every time I speak at the church where I serve, I'm reminded of the power of patience and preseverance. My dad, Kenny Foreman, had a dream to build our current sanctuary. The economy was in a very difficult place back then in the 1970s, but he and the church took a step of faith, bought the property, and started construction with only $37,000 in the bank. He and the

THE CHURCH BUILDING UNDER CONSTRUCTION

church members gave and they sacrificed. The walls started to rise, and then they ran out of money. My dad told the builders to stop construction because he didn't want to owe them what we could not pay. The building sat there for eight months with nothing happening. There were weeds growing up around the outside, and motorcycles used the inside of the building as a track. There were those in the community who called the building "Foreman's Folly."

It was a difficult time. One day, my dad was very discouraged and started driving, but he didn't really have a destination. He was driving down the freeway, not knowing what the church would do, when God dropped a message in his heart. The message was this:

"Mistakes are not fatal, failure is not final, and delays are not denials."

My dad's faith began to rise. He turned the car around and headed back to meet with the staff. He told them he had heard from God and the church would be built.

CATHEDRAL OF FAITH
TODAY

God gave them strength and a strategy, and they started construction again. It was a long journey with lots of twists and turns, starts and stops. But in the spring of 1981, the dream became a realtiy, and the building was finally completed.

Today there are several buildings and an outdoor amphitheater on the 14 acre campus in the heart of Silicon Valley, and thanks to God they are all debt-free. But every time I step into the first building and speak at the four weekend services, I am reminded of the power of patience and perservance to take hold of the promise. Dreams do come to those who wait.

"Mistakes are not fatal, failure is not final, and delays are not denials."

Just ask Kenny Foreman.

SCAN here to watch Pastor Kenny's interview, or go to www.cathedraloffaith.org/kennyforeman

 *reflection*

Waiting Game

1. Think about a moment when you were glad you waited. Perhaps it was a moment when you held your tongue, or held off a decision, or let the other person finish talking. Write about that experience and what you learned.

2. What is the hardest part of "waiting" for you? Write out some things you could do the next time you are "waiting."

3. Pray this prayer: *Heavenly Father, when I reflect on my journey as Your child, there are many times in which You waited patiently for me to turn to You. Give me Your perspective on the circumstances that seem to be taking so long in my life. Increase my patience. Show me Your ways. I stand on the words of Your prophet Isaiah: 'They that wait upon the Lord shall have their strength renewed,' (Isaiah 40:31). Have Your way in me. Amen.*

section V

Section 5:
Royal Ending

"You shall be in charge of my palace, and all my people are to submit to your orders" (Genesis 41:40).

chapter SEVENTEEN

Ready to Roll

"Luck is what happens when preparation meets opportunity."
— Denzel Washington, Award Winning Actor and Director

chapter EIGHTEEN
chapter NINETEEN
chapter TWENTY

A husband called his wife from work in the middle of the afternoon, and said, "Honey, I'm able to get two tickets for the play we talked about seeing. Would you like me to get the tickets?" She said, "Absolutely—go ahead and pick up the tickets! I'll get ready right away." The husband replied, "Go ahead and get ready right away, the tickets are for tomorrow night." The husband wanted to make sure when it was time to go to the play, his wife was prepared — his wife was ready.

It's good to be ready when you're on the way to your God-sized dream.

There will be a window that opens. The window isn't always open, but one day the window will open for you. If you're ready for that moment, you'll see and seize the moment. The open window will take you one step closer to your dream.

You never really know when or how the window will open. You can be confident when God gives you a dream, at some point, the window will open. Be confident. Believe the window will open. Be looking for that window to open. The God who drops a dream in your heart will open the window to that dream. **When the window does open, you want to be ready to see it and seize it.**

That's what happened to Joseph. He had a dream he would one day be a ruler. As we've tracked his journey, we've seen him experience all kinds of twists and turns on the way to his dream and yet, he didn't give up on God. He didn't give up on the dream God gave him.

Then, a window opened up for him. The king had a dream in the night and didn't know what the dream meant. One of the men who worked for the king told him about a young Hebrew who had been in prison with him who was "a servant of the captain of the guard. We told him our dreams, and he interpreted them for us, giving each man the interpretation of his dream" (Genesis 41:12). Maybe this man in prison could help the king as well. The name of the young man was Joseph.

The king summoned Joseph and asked for help in understanding his dream. When the window opened for Joseph, he was ready. He was ready to help the king interpret the dream. He was ready to become a leader for the king; so with an open window, Joseph seized the moment.

On the way to your God-sized dream, it's important to be ready.

"Before everything else, getting ready is the secret of success."
— *Henry Ford*

He makes a good point. If you want to have success when that window is open — being prepared is key!

Being ready applies to the…

Athlete who gets ready for the game.

Job applicants who do their homework for a job interview.

Lawyer who prepares for a case.

Coach who watches film of the next opponent.

BEING READY

Believer who learns how to share her faith.

Musician who practices for a concert.

Couple who decides to marry.

Salesperson who works on his presentation.

Being ready is one of the keys to having success when that window is open.

Ask yourself, "What is the thing I can do to ready myself?"

➣ *Kurt Warner* ➣

We had former NFL MVP quarterback Kurt Warner with us for one of our church services. He's hosting a reality TV show called *The Moment,* and it's all about dreams and having a second chance to follow your dreams.

As Kurt talked about his own journey, he spoke on the importance of being prepared. Early in his career, he had a dream to play in the NFL, yet he was frustrated. The window of opportunity had not yet opened for him. He worked the graveyard shift at a grocery store to pay the bills. Even though he was frustrated, he held onto his dream and kept training hard, and when the window did open, he was ready.

First, the window of opportunity opened for him to play in the Arena Football League. Then, the window opened to play in the NFL European League. Finally, the window opened for him to be in the National Football League. He was the backup quarterback for the St. Louis Rams, but when the window of opportunity opened for him to be the starting quarterback, he was ready. He stepped into that role and went on to have an amazing career. In fact, he went from being a backup quarterback to Superbowl MVP in one season.

When the window opens, you have to be ready.
What can you do to prepare?

MY BROTHER KURT, KURT WARNER, & ME

An old African proverb says, "Tomorrow belongs to the people who prepare for it today."

I watched a television program about one of the biggest retail companies in the world. It was the story within the story that caught my attention. There was a man who started working in the shipping department at one of the stores. He made the most of his opportunity there and he got a promotion. He continued to do his best and this led to another promotion. Again he made the most of that opportunity, always doing his very best at whatever he did. Eventually the founder of the company asked him, "Do you think you can run this company?" The man replied he thought he could and that's just what he did. He went from working in the shipping department to becoming the Chief Executive Officer of one of the biggest retail companies in the world.

Tomorrow belongs to the people who prepare for it today. What can you do today to prepare yourself for your tomorrow?

You cannot borrow your readiness from someone else.

Sure we can borrow another person's car, their money, another's jacket, but there are some things you just cannot borrow. You can't borrow readiness. If you have studied, I can't borrow your brain when I take an exam. If you've practiced playing the piano, I can't borrow your fingers for my recital. If you've been working out, I cannot borrow your fitness.

There is a sign in a doctor's office that reads:

I can't borrow your exercise when I go in for my checkup. When I give an account to God of what I have done with the life He gave me, I can't borrow what you've done with your life.

I used to watch golf but I needed more exercise, so now I watch tennis.

"Each of us will give an account of himself to God" **(Romans 14:12).**

There are certain things in life you just cannot borrow and readiness is one of them. If you're going to be ready, you have to get ready yourself. Prepare for the moment when the window to your dream is open.

What can you do to prepare?

One of my worst nightmares involves not being ready. I've had this nightmare more than once. In it I show up at church and am supposed to speak that day. For one reason or another, I didn't realize I was supposed to speak, and I'm not prepared to speak. I'm in a panic and feeling sick because I'm not ready to speak. When I wake up from that nightmare, what a relief! To not be prepared when you need to be prepared is frightening. I don't want to live that nightmare—you don't want to live that nightmare.

God doesn't want you to live that nightmare. God wants you to live your dream — not your nightmare.

What can you do to help prepare for the moment when the window to your dream opens?

One of the best things you can do to ready yourself for your tomorrow is to develop the connection you have with God today.

Make that connection a priority. Spend time in prayer every day. Spend time daily with the Bible. Make that connection a priority. No one else can make that connection for you—you have to make the connection yourself.

God wants to have a connection with you.

GOD

CONNECTION

RELATIONSHIP

YOU

Don't think of it as a religion, think of it more as a relationship. God invites us into a relationship with Him. As we enter into that relationship, enjoy the relationship and develop the relationship. God has a way of preparing you. God had a way of preparing Joseph, and what God did for him, God can do for you. Develop the connection you have with God today. It is one of the best things you can do for your tomorrow.

On the way to your dream, when that window opens, you will be ready.

Ready to Roll

1. What is the thing you can do to ready yourself? What can you do today to prepare yourself for the day when the window to your dream is open?

2. It's one thing to know what you need to do. It's quite another to actually do it. Set out some dates and times as goals for the action steps you will take to be ready.

DATE/TIME	ACTION

3. Pray this prayer: *Lord of the God-sized dream, I need Your God-sized strength and Your God-sized vision to fulfill Your purpose for my life. You promised that You would show me the way and make the path clear. I want to cooperate with You by doing everything in my power to prepare for the open window You will bring. Even though I can't see everything that is ahead, I want to keep my eyes on You, and whatever the next step should be. Amen.*

chapter EIGHTEEN

chapter SEVENTEEN

chapter EIGHTEEN

Problem Solver

"Determine the thing that can and shall be done, and then we shall find the way."
— Abraham Lincoln, Sixteenth U.S. President

chapter NINETEEN
chapter TWENTY

In a *Peanuts* comic strip, Charlie Brown goes to see Lucy. Lucy is set up in her psychiatrist booth and Charlie Brown asks for some advice. She says, "Do you know what the problem with you is Charlie Brown? The problem with you is that you are you." Charlie Brown replies, "What am I supposed to do about that?" Lucy answers, "I do not pretend to have the solution—I just point out the problem."

It seems almost anyone can point out a **problem**. They can look at a problem, point their finger and say, "There is a problem—we have a problem." Pointing out the problem is the easy part. People who achieve their dreams see more than just the problem. They see the solution to the problem. They think of creative ways the problem can be solved.

On the way to your dream, train yourself to look for solutions. Be a person who is a solution-oriented thinker.

Joseph, our young man in the Bible, was a solution-oriented thinker.

The king told Joseph about his two dreams. In the king's first dream, he saw seven years of abundance. The second dream followed with seven years of famine. The dreams were a forecast for the future economy of not only the king's kingdom, but of all the surrounding countries as well. Since there were two dreams, they believed it was going to happen soon. Joseph pointed out the obvious challenges a coming famine would cause for the king. Then Joseph did something more; he proposed a way of dealing with the challenge.

He suggested, "If we collect the grain during those good years, and store it in your cities until it is needed, this will keep the country from being destroyed because of the lack of food" **(Genesis 41:33-36 CEV).**

He did more than point out the problem; he came up with a solution. Joseph was a problem solver, a solution-oriented thinker.

On the way to your God-sized dream, you will run into some problems.

If you haven't run into them yet, just wait; you will. Everyone has a problem, is a problem, or lives with a problem. On the way to your dream you will run into problems. That's why we need to open our hearts and our minds. We need to ask God to give us creative thoughts, creative ideas, and creative solutions so we can be solution-oriented thinkers. We need solution-oriented thinking.

- Couples need solution-oriented thinking.
- Churches, schools, companies, and communities need solution-oriented thinking.
- Everyone and every organization with a problem needs solution-oriented thinking.

 There is a professor at Stanford who teaches a class on creative thinking. In the class, she gives them a problem to try and solve. She asks her students to line up according to their birthdays, from January 1 to December 31. Here's the catch — there is no talking allowed.

At first, she says the kids kind of freeze and think it's impossible, but then someone will get the process going, and the class will find a way to solve it. In fact, the teacher points out there are many ways they could have solved it. They could have written down their birthdays on paper, they could have pulled out their drivers licenses, they could have created a timeline on the floor, or they would have sung their birthdays—they couldn't talk, but she didn't say they couldn't sing.

I like the fact that she's getting young people to look at problems in new ways. That's how we're going to solve problems — with **solution-oriented thinking.**

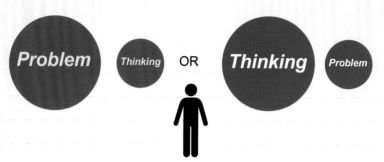

The problem is not that the problem is too big. The problem is our thinking is too small. Be a person who does more than point out the problem. Train yourself to be a person who points out solutions.

I know of a leader who suggests you play a game when you have a problem or a challenge in front of you. The game is called,

"Count to Ten and Win."

He suggests when you have a problem, write down at least ten different solutions to the problem. Turn your Spirit-filled imagination loose and write down at least ten different things that could possibly solve the problem. He has helped a lot of people with this idea because it frees your mind to think creatively. It's easy for your mind to get stuck on the problem. This exercise will help you get stuck on solutions. Also, ask others to help you with your list.

Out of those ten solutions, there may be three best options. One of the three, or a combination of the three, may be put into practice and solve the problem.

1.   6.
2.   7.
3.   8.
4.   9.
5.   10.

The solution is there; we just have to train our minds to get stuck on the solution instead of getting stuck on the problem.

My wife, Alisa, loves paper and pens. If we're at the mall and we walk by a stationery store, I find myself a bench. We're going to be there for a while. I guess it could be worse. She could love jewelry and if she loved jewelry, I might be sleeping on the bench. But, she loves paper and pens and I am thankful to take a seat on the bench. Her favorite kind of pen is a Waterman pen.

The Waterman pen was inspired by a problem.

An insurance salesman was about to make a sale but when he pulled out the pen in his pocket, the pen didn't work. When the pen didn't work, the customer got cold feet. He lost the sale and thought, 'There has to be a better way to make a pen.' So, he went to work on a pen you could depend on, and the Waterman pen is what came out of that problem. It is one of the finest pens you can buy today and it all started with a problem and a person determined to find a solution.

Every problem presents you with an opportunity to come up with a solution. You never know where that solution will take you.

 Problem = Opportunity

When Joseph suggested his solution to the king, the king was impressed. He decided this was the kind of man he needed on his staff. He could see the favor and wisdom of God was with Joseph. The king moved Joseph into the palace and he made him second in command in the country.

He said to Joseph, "I am putting you in charge of the entire country of Egypt" **(Genesis 41:41).**

Joseph started the day in the prison and he ended the day in the palace. That's what you call a promotion.

When you come up with a solution, you never know where that solution will take you.

WITH A NEW INTRODUCTION BY THE AUTHOR

THE

ROAD LESS TRAVELED

25TH ANNIVERSARY EDITION

A New Psychology of Love, Traditional Values and Spiritual Growth

M. SCOTT PECK, M.D.

Dr. Scott Peck says,
"Problems call forth our courage and our wisdom; indeed they create our courage and our wisdom."

When you run into a problem, instead of viewing the problem as a problem, view the problem as an opportunity. View the problem as an opportunity to exercise the creative mind God has given to you. Use your imagination to come up with solutions.

 Problem = Opportunity

One teacher asked her students, if you had ten potatoes and you had to divide them among twelve people, how would you do it?

One child lifted his hand and said, "I would mash them and make mashed potatoes."

There are problems in the world today waiting for someone like you to step up. Instead of simply pointing out the problem, point out solutions to the problem. God can give you the wisdom you need to tackle any problem. When you run into a challenge, don't run away from it. Be confident there is a way through the problem, around the problem or over the problem.

You may not have found the way yet, but with the help of God, you will find a way to defeat the problem.

One of the leading inventors in all of history was **Thomas Edison.** He would have been right at home in the Silicon Valley. Among other things, he dreamed of creating a light bulb that would be practical and safe for use inside of people's homes. According to the Smithsonian, it took Edison over a year and a half and 1,600 tries to find a filament that would work in the bulb. He stuck with it, stayed at it, found a solution, and the light bulb Edison created changed the world.

He once said, "If I find 10,000 ways something won't work, I haven't failed. I am not discouraged, because every wrong attempt discarded is often a step forward."

You may not have found your solution, yet. It may take you 10,000 tries. But, believe every problem has a solution and with the help of God, you can be the one to find it.

Don't let the problem defeat you. Instead determine that you will one day defeat the problem. When you train your mind to dream of solutions, you are on your way to your dream.

 *reflection*

Be a Problem Solver

1. List the roadblocks keeping you from
   the fulfillment of your God-sized dream.

Problems

2. Brainstorm at least ten different solutions to the roadblocks/problems.

3. Pray with me: *God of All-Power, there is nothing too difficult for You. You are greater than any problem. You have the final word on all obstacles that clutter my journey toward the fulfillment of Your dream for my life. Remind me that through Christ's strength, I can do all things. Amen.*

 **chapter NINETEEN**

chapter SEVENTEEN
chapter EIGHTEEN

chapter NINETEEN

Forgive and Forget

"To forgive is to set a prisoner free and discover that the prisoner is you."

— Philip Yancey, Award Winning Author

chapter TWENTY

There is a man named Rick Steves who writes popular travel books. When he travels, all he takes with him is a backpack. When my wife and I travel we take more than a backpack. We have bags on our backs and on our shoulders and in our hands and in our teeth. We travel with all kinds of baggage. When Rick Steves travels, he travels with just a backpack. I suggest on your way to your dream, you learn to travel the way he travels. Learn to travel light. If you carry around baggage like resentment and bitterness, it is a heavy load. It will wear you out, wear you down, and keep you from reaching your dream. Even if you do reach your dream carrying around all of that baggage, the resentment and bitterness will keep you from enjoying your dream.

 One expert **Lewis Smedes**, says this about the baggage we carry, "You will never be a happy person until you learn to let go of resentment."

It is hard to enjoy the present when you have not let go of the past.

Lady Gaga is adored by millions of people. She is on the top of *Forbes Magazine*'s list of most powerful people in the world. And yet, she is still haunted by the pain of the past. In one interview with the *New York Times*, she opened a window into her soul. When she was younger, she was called really horrible names in front of large groups of people. She had been a good student in school but there came a point that she didn't even want to go to class. Even today, she carries that hurt and pain with her. Her closest friends have told her everything is great, that she's a singer and her dreams came true. And yet Lady Gaga says, **"When certain things are said over and over again as you're growing up, it stays with you."**

It is hard to enjoy your dream when you still carry around the pain of the past.

On the way to your God-sized dream let go of all that baggage and learn how to travel light. This is what Joseph learned to do. He learned how to travel light. Remember, Joseph had been wronged many times. He had many reasons to carry bitterness and resentment but he decided to travel light.

When Joseph eventually married and had children, he chose the name Manasseh for his first son. In those days, names had meanings and often carried a special message.

Manasseh means "God has made me forget." Joseph had a lot to forget! Joseph was hurt many times, and by many people, starting with his family.

The people you love the most are the people who can hurt you the most. When you have been hurt like that, it is very hard to forget. The wound can be deep and you can end up carrying around the baggage of bitterness and resentment as you travel.

Before you finish reading this chapter, go find a piece of luggage, briefcase or backpack and hold it on your lap. Once you've got the baggage in place, keep reading.

With the help of God, Joseph chose to forgive those who had hurt him along the way, even those who had hurt him the most — his family. He eventually met up with the brothers who had hurt him. His brothers were afraid because they thought he would take revenge on them for what they had done. Instead, Joseph told his brothers they had nothing to fear from him because he had forgiven them for what they had done to him. He ended up blessing them in spite of their actions. What they had done was wrong and there was no excuse for it.

Yet he told them, "Even though you planned evil against me, God planned good to come out of it" **(Genesis 50:20 GWT).**

> ## He harbored no resentment. On the way to his dream, Joseph learned the secret of traveling light.
> ## On the way to your dream, do yourself a favor and learn the secret of traveling light. Carrying around all that baggage is not good for you.

While we all know cigarette smoking can have a negative effect on your health, and we regularly hear about the harmful effects of a high fat diet on your body, a clinical study found bitterness and resentment are just as bad for your health. If you carry around bitterness and resentment, it can cut short your life in the same way cigarette smoking can cut short your life, in the same way a high fat diet can cut short your life.

Carrying around baggage can cut short your life.

We need to write in big letters on the side of all this baggage:

> *Warning:*
> *Carrying this around is hazardous to your health.*

On the way to your God-sized dream, do yourself a favor and learn the secret of traveling light.

Travel light; refuse to carry baggage from the past.

Maybe you want to forgive, but you are not sure how to let go. Here are a few ideas to help loosen your grip and drop those bags. It starts when you make a decision to forgive. It is a choice you make. You don't excuse what was done or ignore what was done or condone what was done. What was done to you was wrong—that's the reason it needs to be forgiven.

You take the wrong that was done and say,

"WHAT WAS DONE TO ME WAS WRONG AND WHAT WAS DONE TO ME CAUSED A LOT OF HURT. WHAT WAS DONE TO ME CAUSED A LOT OF PAIN, BUT WITH THE HELP OF GOD, I'M MAKING A DECISION IN MY HEART OF HEARTS TO LET GO OF THE BITTERNESS. LET GO OF THE RESENT- MENT AND FORGIVE THE WRONG THAT WAS DONE."

It starts with a decision you make.

Can you see yourself letting go of that baggage?

When someone hurts me, (hard to believe someone would hurt a person as nice as me, but it does happen) the first thing I feel like doing is hurting them back. I want to hurt them as much as they hurt me. And yet what I have learned, (and am still learning) is to take my right to strike back and to turn that right over to God—to trust Him enough that, at the end of the day, He is the one who will make things right. I don't have to try to get even. Every time that I try to get even, it's hard to know where even is. I feel my pain more than I feel your pain, and it is hard to know where even is. That's why we should leave the 'getting even' to God. He knows where even is.

We take our right to strike back, turn it over to Him and trust that He will settle the score.

The Bible says don't try to get even. Leave room for God to show His anger. It is written, "I am the one who judges people. I will pay them back, says the Lord" **(Romans 12:19).**

Can you see yourself letting go of the bag?

 # Then, refuse to dwell on the past.

> One husband said to his wife, "Why do you continue to bring up the past? I thought you had forgiven and forgotten." The wife said, "I have forgiven and forgotten; I just don't want you to forget I have forgiven and forgotten."

When it comes to the past, it may not be possible to forget it, but it is possible not to dwell on it.

When the memories of the past rise up, you have a choice to make. You can dwell on them, playing them over and over in your mind and relive the bad feelings. Or you can take charge of your thoughts. You can refuse to dwell on the past. The past is the past, and you cannot change it.

Say, **I am going to forgive the past and focus my mind on a bright future.**

Even if you never forget the past, that memory will have less power and should show up less often.

One psychologist, **Archibald Hart**, puts it this way, "The memory may be there, but the sting is gone."

➡ Finally, respond in the opposite spirit.

Jesus once said, "Do good to those who hate you, bless those who curse you, pray for those who mistreat you" (Luke 6:27-28).

This is what one little girl did in the 1960s. The focus of the entire nation was on this six-year-old child as she made her way to school. Ruby was the first little girl of a different race to attend this school. While simply walking to school, she encountered an angry crowd calling her names. Imagine how difficult that must have been for her at such a young age.

RUBY BRIDGES

During that time, her schoolteacher watched through the window daily as the kindergartner made her way to the classroom. The teacher said she noticed the girl's lips were moving when she was walking through the militant crowd. What had she been saying? The little girl said she was praying for them, asking God to forgive them because they didn't know what they were doing.

When you bless those who curse you, can you see yourself letting go of that bag?

Learn to travel light, without resentment and bitterness. It will make for a happier, easier journey on the way to reaching your dream.

 *reflection*

Forgive and Forget

1. Ask God to show you if there is anyone you need to forgive. It may be a recent offense or a deep wound from years past. Write down their names in this space.

2. Go back and read through the four steps of forgiveness with each person in mind. In this space write down the ways God may be asking you to bless them.

3. Pray this prayer: *Lord, You are my Savior and Redeemer. There is no sin I have committed You will not forgive. Give me the strength to be forgiving and leave behind any baggage of bitterness or unforgiveness that would keep me from moving forward. I cannot do this in my own strength. I know freedom comes from You. Amen.*

 **chapter TWENTY**

chapter TWENTY

Keep
Planting
Seeds

"Dreams are the seeds of change. Nothing
ever grows without a seed, and nothing
ever changes without a dream."

— **Debby Boone,** Grammy Award Winning Singer

A high school teacher with 20 years dedicated to her career had a new dream to help the poor. Her fellow teachers described her as an average person. Yet, this God-sized dream dropped into the heart of this average person, and she reached out to help the poor. She started by helping one poor person, then another needy person, and another. She helped scores of poor people as she

stuck with her dream. One day someone was watching her live her dream and said to her, "I wouldn't do that for a million dollars!"

She smiled at him and said, "I wouldn't do it for a million dollars, either, but I will do it for Jesus."

That average high school teacher with a God-sized dream was **Mother Teresa**.

Follow the dream God drops in your heart— you just never know how big that dream will end up being.

He can do more than we can ask or even imagine.

This is what happened to our young man in the Bible, Joseph. He had a dream dropped in his heart to be a leader, but he never realized just how big the dream would end up being. He became the second most powerful man in the world. He then used the position and power he had to save and improve the lives of others. Because of his leadership and the wisdom of his plan to prepare for the famine, he saved the lives of his family, the lives of those in his country, and the lives of those in the countries around him.

Who could have imagined this one man and his dream would have such an impact on his world? When he looked at what God did in and through him, he named his second son Ephraim, meaning "God has made him fruitful" **(Genesis 41:52 NLT).**

When you follow your dream you never know how big that dream will end up being.

God can do "much more than we ask or imagine" **(Ephesians 3:20).**

We had a dream as a church to help feed the needy families in our San Jose community. We followed that dream and began to give out a few bags of groceries from a closet each weekend. Over time and with God's help, He expanded what we are able to do.

We now have a **16,000 square foot building** that is filled with food.

We serve **over 120,000 people a year.**

In 2012, at Christmas alone, we gave **3,000 families over $700,000 worth of food**.

It has grown into one of the largest food distribution programs in the entire state. It is amazing to see what God has done. It all started in a closet, following a dream to serve the poor. You never know how big that dream will end up being.

God can do much more than we can ask or imagine.

My dad has a saying, "Anyone can count the seeds in an apple but only God can count the apples in a seed that is planted."

When you have a dream and you follow that dream, it's like a seed is planted. It may seem like one seed can't do very much, achieve very much, or accomplish very much. But if you plant a seed in the ground, with the blessing of God, that one seed can produce much more than you can imagine. You can end up with a whole basket of apples in your hands. You just never know what God can do with one seed. You never know what God can do with one dream. He can bless it and multiply it until the branches of that dream are filled with fruit. He will make your life fruitful and make your dream fruitful. He just needs someone who will step up, plant a seed, and follow a dream. That person can be you.

God can do much more than we can ask or imagine.

Joseph said, "God has made me fruitful in the land of my suffering" **(Genesis 41:52).**

That is the amazing thing about God. He can make you fruitful in the very place where you have had so much pain and suffering.

I have a friend who worked for a major company in the Silicon Valley. After years of service, he felt he was treated unfairly when he was laid off from the company. It was a very painful experience for him to walk through. After a few years, the door opened back up for him to do some work for that same company. At first, it wasn't easy for him to head back to the place where there had been so much pain. But the door opened, he went back to work in the same location and ended up making more money with them than he had ever made before.

He was fruitful in the very place that had been so painful.

Not only can God make you prosper, He can make you prosper in the place that had been so difficult for you.

Another man in the Bible by the name of Peter had let down his very best friend, Jesus. When Jesus needed Peter the most he denied he even knew Jesus. Three times he denied he knew Jesus. It was a very painful memory for Peter, a very painful experience. Yet a few weeks later Peter was in the same city. This time he took a stand for his friend Jesus. **He told others about his friend Jesus and then led 3,000 people to put their faith and trust in his friend Jesus.** In the same place that had been so painful for him, God had made him fruitful. What God did for him God can do for you.

In the place that has been so painful for you, God can make you fruitful. Anyone can count the seeds in an apple but only God can count the apples in a seed.

In fact, there are times that pain can make your life more fruitful, and add more apples to the tree. Imagine a tree getting pruned each year. No branch likes the shears, shears have a sharp edge to them (ouch!). But in the right hands, the shears can make your life even more fruitful.

Maybe some things need to be cut away from your life so you and your dream can be more fruitful than ever.

Maybe there is a relationship keeping you from being more fruitful.

Perhaps it is an attitude or habit keeping you from being more fruitful.

If you will bring that branch to God and ask Him to prune what needs to be pruned, He will make you and your dream even more fruitful. You never know just what He can do. When you follow your dream,

God can do much more than we can ask or imagine.

Anyone can count the seeds in an apple, but only God can count the apples in a seed.

⇒ David Pack ⇐

DAVID PACK

My friend David Pack has had a fruitful life in so many ways. When he was young he had a dream to write a hit song and he ended up writing several. He went on to become a Grammy Award-winning singer, songwriter, and producer. He was the lead singer for the band Ambrosia and has created some amazing music. Over the course of his career, he has written songs such as *Biggest Part of Me.* He has produced important events including Presidential Inaugural Balls, created video tributes for leaders such as Billy Graham, and worked on benefit projects with Rick Warren. His life and his career have been fruitful in so many ways, well beyond what he could imagine. One inspiring song he wrote is called, *The Secret of Movin' On.* It's a song about forgiveness and letting go of the resentment of the past so you can take hold of the future. The secret of moving on is traveling light. I recommend downloading and playing it over and over again. It's the kind of song that, if it gets in your head and it gets in your heart, God can use the song to set you free from your past so you can take hold of your future.

David told me that while he was getting ready to play a special event, the organizer of the evening asked him if he would perform *The Secret of Movin' On.* The young lady who organized the private event said it was very important she speak alone to him after sound-check. She then told him, while in tears and trembling, how one night only a few years prior, she sat alone in her car, prepared to take her own life out of desperation, sadness, and anger over many things that happened in her life she considered "unforgivable." Someone had given her David's CD that opened with the title song *The Secret of Movin' On* and told her to listen to it. Through tears, she told David she played the song more than 20 times and felt God spoke to her through the song.

She made a decision to live... and to forgive. She hired David for the event just so she could make sure and thank him for saving her life through this song.

The secret David sings about is the song's sub-title *Travelin' Light*, that can only come about when you've forgiven someone and released yourself from the baggage and weight of carrying resentment around. True forgiveness frees us to take hold of the future. Sometimes God can use a song to open a closed heart. *The Secret of Movin' On* was fruitful in ways David Pack couldn't even imagine. He didn't know when he dreamed of the song and performed it, God would use the dream to help this woman and many others. It's never just about you. It is about more than you.

God can make your life more fruitful than you could ever imagine.

So, what are you waiting for? Live your dream.

SCAN here to hear David perform *The Secret of Movin' On*, or go to www.cathedraloffaith.org/davidpack

reflection

Keep Planting Seeds

1. List some of the areas in which you have already experienced fruitfulness, blessing, and favor of the Lord.

2. We read the words of Jesus in John 15:1-2, "I am the true vine, and my Father is the gardener. He cuts off every branch in me that bears no fruit, while every branch that does bear fruit he prunes so that it will be even more fruitful." Write out any areas God may be pruning in your life.

3. Pray this prayer: *Lord of the Harvest, you are the giver of all good things. You are working all things for good in my life. I thank You for all the ways You have watched over my life and brought me this far. I can't begin to imagine all that You have in store. I will give You all the glory and honor for what You have done. Lead the way. I am following. Amen.*

Epilogue ➡

Epilogue

Take A Leap of Faith

"Every man dies; not every man really lives."
— Braveheart

There's a riddle that goes like this—if there are eight frogs sitting on the log and six of them are getting ready to jump, how many frogs are left on the log? The answer is eight, because getting ready to jump is not the same thing as jumping.

➣ *my story* ➢

For a long time, that is where I was — stuck on that log. God put a dream in my heart to write a book. Others told me I should write a book. When I went to a place to speak, they would ask me to bring the books I had written. I would bring a box with me; the box was empty. I had not written any books.

For one reason or another, I had a dream in my heart, but that's where the dream stayed. I never took any action on it. I never took a step of faith toward it. For a long time I was stuck on that log with the rest of the frogs.

Then one day, I took a leap of faith and jumped toward that dream. There were lots of twists on the way to the dream. That's usually how dreams work. It's a little bit like playing a round of golf. I play golf, and I know most of the time, golf is not about straight lines. Pro golfer Lee Trevino once said, "I'm in the woods so much I can tell you which plants are edible." Golf is not about straight lines. It's about being in the trees, the fairway, a sand trap—but eventually, you're on the green and in the hole. (As long as you don't throw your clubs in the lake.)

Dreams are a lot like golf—going in a straight line just doesn't happen, but eventually, you will get there. So I started writing, and rewriting, and researching. I went in one direction, then another. I hit a few sand traps, and landed in a few trees. Somehow I managed to keep my clubs out of the lake, and press on.

That dream, which was once only in my heart, is now on these pages.
I now have one book to put in a box when I travel.

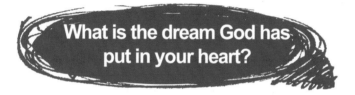

What is the dream God has put in your heart?

Believe in the dream He has put in your heart. Take a step of faith toward that dream. It may be a dream you have for your ...

CAREER MARRIAGE FINANCES HEALTH

OVERCOMING OF AN ADDICTION COMMUNITY MINISTRY

You have a dream in your heart, but for one reason or another, you have been stuck on the log. Take a step of faith toward the dream — there is always a step of faith you can take —

go ahead and jump!

Sometimes the first step is the hardest one to take. I know how easy it is to get stuck and stay stuck on that log. That log can be comfortable. But there is a God-sized dream out there just waiting for you to live it.

It takes a step of faith, not a step of facts, to get started.

When you start toward your dream, you never have all the facts. You never know all of the twists or turns ahead of you. If you wait until you have all the facts to get started toward your dream, you will never get started. It's an illusion to think you can ever have all the facts. To step toward your dream is a step of faith, not a step of facts.

You took a risk when…

- You got in the car and drove on the freeway.

- You got on your computer and went on-line.

- You ate lunch at a restaurant.

  (You didn't see the chef cook your food. You didn't see where the food came from. That is why you should never be mean to your waiter.)

Everything is risky. When you take a step of faith toward your God-sized dream, it will feel risky. If you love taking risks, this may excite you. If you hate taking risks, this may terrify you. Either way, there is this dream out there waiting to be lived. Take that step and follow your dream.

We only get one life and it seems to go by very fast. When I get to the end of my life, I don't want to look back and see a dream God put in my heart that I never even tried to pursue. I may not reach all of my dreams, but I don't want to come to the end of my life, look back, and wish I would have taken a leap of faith and followed a dream.

> They once surveyed people who were over 90 years old and asked them, "If you had your life to live over again, what would you do differently?"
>
> One of the things at the top of their list was they wished they had taken more risks.

Following a dream feels risky, but don't stay stuck on the log - just take a leap of faith and live that dream. Even if you don't reach or achieve all your dreams, at least give it your best shot.

Rick Warren says what he wants put on his tombstone is, "At least I tried." With your one shot in life, give life your best shot.

What is keeping you from taking a leap of faith?

I was talking with a young lady who once had a dream to become a model. She was in an abusive relationship at the time, and the man she was with crushed that dream in her heart. But recently the dream has started to stir once again. The dream is alive and she's taking a step of faith toward that dream. She doesn't know exactly how far the dream will take her or where the dream will end up, but when she looks back at her life she wants to know she did follow the dream.

If your dream has been crushed, dormant, or even died, life can come back into that dream. You can take a step toward it. With your one shot at life, give life your best shot, and at the end of the day, that's what matters most.

Never outlive your dreams.

If you've had a dream in the past, dream a new dream for the future and take a step of faith toward that dream. Think about Joseph—he lived the dream of being a leader, but he had another dream.

Joseph dreamed one day his family would move back to the promised land. He dreamed they would live in the land God promised him and his family. He knew he wouldn't live to see that dream come to pass, but it didn't mean he passed on that dream. He took hold of the dream that would outlive him and he left these instructions:

"When that day comes, when we leave this country, when we head back to that land, make sure to take my bones with you" **(Genesis 50:25 NLT).**

He didn't outlive his dreams—his dreams outlived him. He believed in those dreams, and one day, his dream did come true. Never outlive your dreams. Believe in those dreams and take a step of faith to follow them.

My wife and I were in Florence, Italy and visited The Basilica di Santa Maria del Fiore, a church over 600 years old. When they first built the church, they left a hole in the top. That isn't how we build churches today, with a hole in the top. But this church—they left a hole in the top because they didn't have the technology at the time to build a dome to cover the hole. They had a dream to build the church and believed a person would one day figure out how to build the dome.

They took a step of faith and built the church before they had the dome. And they were right—a person did figure out how to build the dome and the domed church still stands today, a reminder dreams can happen.

Dreams can happen for those who are willing to take a step of faith. There is a dream waiting for you to follow.

The picture on the cover of the book is of me skydiving. I decided to do this as a way to open a sermon on taking a leap of faith (or maybe it was just a mid-life crisis). I went through the training, climbed on the plane, and at 14,000 feet in the air, it was time to jump. As I moved toward the door, I felt like my heart was about to come out of my chest. As I stood at the door and looked outside, I thought I was going to be sick. As a tandem dive, there was someone there to give me a nudge and take that leap of faith, and when I did, it was one of the most amazing experiences. Free falling for 90 seconds, feeling the wind in your face, soaring 100 miles per hour through the sky — it was what we used to call back in the day *a total rush.* But that experience wouldn't have happened if I didn't jump. Maybe the reason I was supposed to write this book was to give you that gentle nudge out the door toward your dream — to take that leap of faith. See yourself on the cover of the book.

Go ahead and jump!

Look at today's date. Mark it. Memorize it. Let this be the birthday of God's dream for you, where God wants you to start today— a new beginning, a fresh start, a wondrous dream that's all yours.

LIVE YOUR DREAM!

Scan here to watch my skydive and sermon, or go to www.cathedraloffaith.org/skydiving

⇒ A Personal Note ⇐

Thank you for picking up this book and taking the time to read it. There is a dream on the inside of you waiting to get out. I hope this book has inspired and encouraged you. Wherever you are on your spiritual journey, the most important thing I could ever do in this book is point you to Jesus. You will find plenty of evidence that shows Jesus is who He says He is and can do what He says He will do. Jesus said, "I came so they can have real and eternal life, more and better life than they ever dreamed of "(John 10:10 MSG). Jesus has done this for me. He can do it for you. In fact, you can begin the dream of your life with Him, by praying this prayer:

Jesus, I put my faith and my trust in You. I believe you are the Savior of the world and I surrender my life to You. Thank you for forgiving me of my past, giving me power for my present, and giving me a hope for my future. Amen.

Becoming a follower of Jesus is the most important decision you will ever make in your life. If you prayed that prayer, I would love to hear from you and send you some materials to get you started on this dream journey with Jesus. Contact us at **cathedraloffaith.org** or call us at **408-267-4691** and let us know you have made a decision to follow Jesus, and we will get those helpful resources to you.

The dream for your life is really just starting.

Ken Foreman

⋟ *The Dream Lives On* ⋞

This is a 'living book'—growing and evolving as time passes and more people discover the dream God has for them. I want to know what dream God has planted in your heart. Videotape your story and upload it to YouTube. Email me the link at imagine@cathedraloffaith.org. We will take your link and put some of the stories we receive on our website. You can see these stories at www.cathedraloffaith.org/imagine. It is our hope people will be encouraged by how others are living out their dreams.

And finally, I know there's so much more to be said about dreams, so I'm including a QR code you can scan to discover a new **Dream Tip**, updated quarterly. You'll hear from myself and my Dream Team at the Cathedral of Faith in San Jose, CA. You just never know who might turn up sharing their Dream Tip — the possibilities are endless — just like the dreams God has for your life.

www.cathedraloffaith.org/livingbook

Remember, everything starts with a dream.

Use *Imagine Living Your Dream* for Study

This book is an excellent resource for one-on-one discipleship or small group study. If you are coaching, mentoring, or discipling another person, make a plan to connect once a week and go through the book a chapter at a time. If you have a small group, life group, class, or study group meeting weekly, plan to gather and share one chapter at a time. When you meet together, share:

1. Which quote, thought, idea or picture in this chapter helped you most to move forward with God's dream this week?
2. Share something you wrote down in the chapter that was very meaningful to you.
3. What do you need to let go of from the past or change now in your life to move forward with your dream?
4. What can you identify with in the life of Joseph that helps you better understand what God is doing in your life right now?
5. Share a prayer need with your partner or group.
6. Pray for one another; make a prayer list to pray during the coming week.
7. Decide what chapter you will work on for the coming week and when you will meet again.

Remember to keep confidential what is shared and do not force anyone to disclose anything they don't feel comfortable sharing. The goal of reading and studying this resource together with a partner or a group is to encourage one another and pray for one another as each person lives out his or her dream from God.

Great Resources

The following are wonderful resources from many of the folks you have read about in this book. I recommend them!

Grace Hill Media
www.gracehillmedia.com

Little Angels
www.littleangels.com/roma

The Bible Mini Series
www.thebibleminiseries.com/

David Pack Music
www.davidpack.com

Bruce Wilkinson Ministries
www.brucewilkinson.com

Kurt Warner's First Things First Foundation
www.kurtwarner.org

The Word of Promise Audio Bible with Jim Caviezel
www.thewordofpromise.com

Donnie Moore Ministries
www.donniemooreministries.org

Anointed - Steve Crawford and Da'dra Greathouse
anointedonline.org

The Cathedral of Faith, San Jose, CA
www.cathedraloffaith.org

University Preparatory Academy
www.upasv.org

Dave Ramsey - Financial Peace University
www.daveramsey.com/fpu

Dr. Larry Keefauver
Write the Book... Leave a Legacy in Print!
www.ymcs.org

Harvest Evangelism and
The International Transformation Network
www.transformourworld.org